Student Workbook

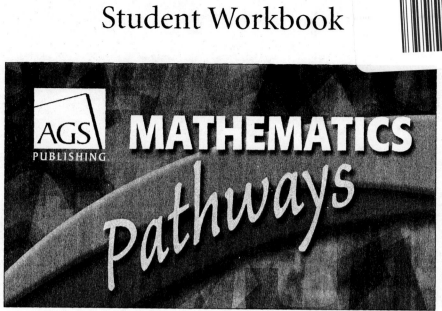

AGS\ MATHEMATICS
PUBLISHING
Pathways

AGS Publishing
Circle Pines, MN 55014-1796
800-328-2560

© 2004 AGS Publishing
4201 Woodland Road
Circle Pines, MN 55014-1796
800-328-2560 • www.agsnet.com

AGS Publishing is a trademark and trade name of American Guidance Service, Inc.

Printed in the United States of America

ISBN 0-7854-3606-5

Product Number 93873

V036 10 9 8 7 6 5

Table of Contents

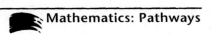

The Base 10 System

EXAMPLE	Compare the equations. Use the < or > signs.

$$6H + 2T + 3TT \underline{\hspace{1cm}} 6H + 1T + 4TT$$

Step 1 $6H + 2T + 3TT = 600 + 2,000 + 30,000$

$600 + 2,000 + 30,000 = 32,600$

Step 2 $6H + 1T + 4TT = 600 + 1,000 + 40,000$

$600 + 1,000 + 40,000 = 41,600$

Step 3 $32,000 < 41,600$

H =   10 TENS

T =   100 TENS

TT = 1,000 TENS

Directions   Compare the equations. Use the < or > signs.

1. $2H + 4T + 8TT \underline{\hspace{1.5cm}} 9H + 2T + 4TT$

2. $7H + 0T + 3TT \underline{\hspace{1.5cm}} 7H + 3TT + 0TT$

3. $0H + 1T + 1TT \underline{\hspace{1.5cm}} 1H + 0T + 0TT$

4. $5H + 2T + 6TT \underline{\hspace{1.5cm}} 7H + 1T + 5TT$

5. $9H + 0T + 6TT \underline{\hspace{1.5cm}} 9H + 9T + 0TT$

6. $2H + 3T + 4TT \underline{\hspace{1.5cm}} 4H + 3T + 2TT$

7. $7H + 3T + 6TT \underline{\hspace{1.5cm}} 3H + 8T + 6TT$

Directions   Fill in the blanks.

8. $9H = \underline{\hspace{1.5cm}}$ TENS

9. $6T = \underline{\hspace{1.5cm}}$ TENS

10. 400 TENS $= \underline{\hspace{1.5cm}}$

11. $5H = \underline{\hspace{1.5cm}}$ TENS

12. $3TT = \underline{\hspace{1.5cm}}$ TENS

13. 40 TENS $= \underline{\hspace{1.5cm}}$

14. $4,000$ TENS $= \underline{\hspace{1.5cm}}$

15. $2T = \underline{\hspace{1.5cm}}$ TENS

Place Value

EXAMPLE Add or subtract the numbers written as powers of ten.

$10^6 + 10^3$

Step 1 $10^6 = 1,000,000$

Step 2 $10^3 = 1,000$

Step 3 $1,000,000 + 1,000 = 1,001,000$

Directions The numbers are written as powers of ten. Add or subtract.

1. $10^4 + 10^6 =$ _____

2. $10^1 + 10^5 =$ _____

3. $10^2 + 10^5 =$ _____

4. $10^4 + 10^3 =$ _____

5. $10^2 + 10^1 =$ _____

6. $10^5 + 10^0 =$ _____

7. $10^1 - 10^0 =$ _____

8. $10^0 - 10^0 =$ _____

9. $10^6 - 10^3 =$ _____

10. $10^3 - 10^1 =$ _____

Directions Round and estimate.

A car can travel 749 more miles before an oil change.

11. Day 1: 263 miles = _____ miles total

12. Day 2: 225 miles = _____ miles total

13. Day 3: 118 miles = _____ miles total

14. Day 4: 62 miles = _____ miles total

Is it time for an oil change? Add the estimates, and find the total number of miles.

15. Total = _____ miles

Addition and Subtraction

EXAMPLE   Rewrite in vertical form.
Identify the place value that requires regrouping.
Solve each problem, and use the inverse operation to check the answer.

$$621 - 350$$

Step 1 $\begin{array}{r} 621 \\ -\,350 \\ \hline \end{array}$

Step 2 $\begin{array}{r} 621 \\ -\,350 \\ \hline \end{array}$

Step 3 $\begin{array}{r} 621 \\ -\,350 \\ \hline 271 \end{array}$ $\begin{array}{r} 350 \\ +\,271 \\ \hline 621 \end{array}$

Directions   Rewrite in vertical form. Solve, then use the inverse operation to check your answer.

1. $226 + 318$

2. $811 - 219$

3. $605 + 76$

4. $912 - 52$

5. $1{,}267 + 416$

6. $930 - 211$

7. $737 + 1{,}205$

8. $212 + 89$

9. $543 + 294$

10. $715 + 228$

11. $1{,}011 - 900$

12. $841 - 750$

13. $566 + 350$

14. $190 + 11$

15. $632 - 442$

16. $931 + 251$

17. $438 - 62$

18. $983 + 18$

19. $375 - 80$

20. $606 + 400$

Multiplication and Division

EXAMPLE Write and solve two problems. Use the solution to the first problem in the second problem.

22 and 5

Step 1 22×5

Step 2 $22 \times 5 = 110$

Step 3 $110 \div 22 = 5$

Directions Write and solve two problems.

1. 36 and 4   _____

2. 70 and 7   _____

3. 41 and 3   _____

4. 4 and 5   _____

5. 594 and 6   _____

6. 56 and 2   _____

7. 126 and 9   _____

8. 28 and 7   _____

9. 100 and 5   _____

10. 135 and 15   _____

11. 200 and 10   _____

12. 12 and 2   _____

13. 64 and 4   _____

14. 72 and 9   _____

15. 123 and 3   _____

The Base 2 System

EXAMPLE Compare the numbers. Use the < and > signs.

$$110_2 \underline{\quad\quad} 34_{10}$$

Step 1 $110_2 = 6$

Step 2 $34_{10} = 34$

Step 3 $6 < 34$

Directions Compare the numbers. Use the < and > signs.

1. 11111_2 _____ 60_{10}

2. 1110_2 _____ 25_{10}

3. 100_2 _____ 100_{10}

4. 111_2 _____ 51_{10}

5. 10_2 _____ 1_{10}

6. 10001_2 _____ 95_{10}

7. 1111_2 _____ 10_{10}

8. 1010_2 _____ 4_{10}

9. 1000_2 _____ 2_{10}

10. 11_2 _____ 5_{10}

11. 110_2 _____ 76_{10}

12. 1001_2 _____ 48_{10}

13. 10111_2 _____ 22_{10}

14. 10010_2 _____ 62_{10}

15. 1100_2 _____ 89_{10}

The Base 5 System

EXAMPLE Find the pattern, and fill in the blank.

$66, 76, 321_5,$ _____

Step 1 $321_5 = (3 \times 25) + (2 \times 5) + (1 \times 1)$

Step 2 $(3 \times 25) + (2 \times 5) + (1 \times 1) = 75 + 10 + 1 = 86$

Step 3 $66, 76, \mathbf{86}, \underline{96}$

Directions Find the pattern, and fill in the blank. Write the answers in base 10 form.

1. $22, 101_5, 30,$ _____

2. $120_5, 30,$ _____ $, 20$

3. $100, 125,$ _____ $, 1200_5$

4. $2, 4_5, 6,$ _____

5. $42,$ _____ $, 143_5, 51$

6. $9, 33_5,$ _____ $, 36$

7. $2000_5,$ _____ $, 150, 100$

Directions: Write the base 10 numbers in Problems 1–7 in base 5 form.

8. _____

9. _____

10. _____

11. _____

12. _____

13. _____

14. _____

Directions Write 15,625 in base 5 form.

15. _____

Adding Whole Numbers

EXAMPLE   Combine like places when adding.

$$\begin{array}{r} 1 \\ 47 \\ + 28 \\ \hline 5 \end{array}$$ Add the ones. Regroup. $$\begin{array}{r} 1 \\ 17a \\ + 39a \\ \hline 6a \end{array}$$ Add the ones. Regroup.

$$\begin{array}{r} 1 \\ 47 \\ + 28 \\ \hline 75 \end{array}$$ Add the tens. Check. $28 + 47 = 75$ $$\begin{array}{r} 1 \\ 17a \\ + 39a \\ \hline 56a \end{array}$$ Add the tens. Check. $39a + 17a = 56a$

Directions   Write each problem in vertical form. Then solve it by adding.

1. $32 + 28$

tens	ones

2. $23 + 49$

tens	ones

3. $297a + 39a$

hundreds	tens	ones	letters

4. $1,238x + 246x + 99x$

thousands	hundreds	tens	ones	letters

5. $943b + 644b + 86b$

thousands	hundreds	tens	ones	letters

Directions   Add the following addends. Show how to check each problem.

     Check   **Check**   **Check**

6. $$\begin{array}{r} 44 \\ + 17 \\ \hline \end{array}$$

10. $$\begin{array}{r} 38b \\ 467b \\ + 877b \\ \hline \end{array}$$

13. $$\begin{array}{r} 1,412y \\ 391y \\ + 2,744y \\ \hline \end{array}$$

7. $$\begin{array}{r} 91 \\ + 89 \\ \hline \end{array}$$

11. $$\begin{array}{r} 312a \\ 29a \\ + 443a \\ \hline \end{array}$$

14. $$\begin{array}{r} 27 \\ 4,281 \\ + 916 \\ \hline \end{array}$$

8. $$\begin{array}{r} 77x \\ + 139x \\ \hline \end{array}$$

12. $$\begin{array}{r} 808 \\ 913 \\ + 97 \\ \hline \end{array}$$

15. $$\begin{array}{r} 2,491z \\ 3,647z \\ + 244z \\ \hline \end{array}$$

9. $$\begin{array}{r} 311 \\ + 109 \\ \hline \end{array}$$

Subtracting Whole Numbers

EXAMPLE

Sometimes when subtracting, you will need to rename.

To check a subtraction problem, use addition.

		Rename	Check
		2 14	
14	17x	$\cancel{3}$ $\cancel{4}$	18
− 8	− 12x	− 1 6	+ 16
6	5x	1 8	34

Directions Write each problem in vertical form. Then subtract.

1. $27 - 14$

2. $56 - 22$

3. $84 - 31$

4. $77y - 42y$

5. $45c - 39c$

6. $63 - 27$

7. $144 - 28$

8. $233 - 118$

9. $750b - 243b$

10. $912c - 728c$

11. $1{,}874y - 678y$

12. $3{,}135a - 2{,}679a$

Directions Subtract. Then show how to check each problem.

Check

13.   37
    − 16

14.   142x
    − 87x

15.   421
   − 277

Check

16.   325c
    − 66c

17.   291y
    − 36y

18. 1,044b
    − 426b

Check

19. 3,131z
  − 1,967z

20. 5,416a
    − 879a

Estimating Sums and Differences

EXAMPLE   Use an estimate to check whether a sum or a difference makes sense.
To estimate, look at the numeral next to the greatest place value.

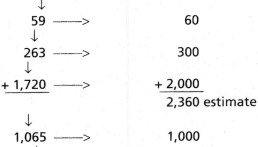

Round up if the numeral is
5 or more.

$\downarrow$
59 ———> 60
$\downarrow$
263 ———> 300
$\downarrow$
+ 1,720 ———> + 2,000
2,360 estimate

Round down if the numeral
is less than 5.

$\downarrow$
1,065 ———> 1,000
$\downarrow$
– 237 ———> – 200
800 estimate

Directions Round each number to the greatest place value.

1. 67 _____

2. 136 _____

3. 241 _____

4. 1,047 _____

5. 2,668 _____

6. 362 _____

7. 5,187 _____

8. 488 _____

9. 237 _____

10. 551 _____

11. 8,125 _____

12. 654 _____

13. 5,871 _____

14. 453 _____

15. 9,412 _____

Directions Estimate each sum. Use rounding. Then find the exact sum.

16. $64 + 87 =$

17. $252 + 524 =$

18. $714 + 892 =$

19. $1,561 + 243 =$

20. $3,821 + 451 =$

Directions Estimate each difference. Use rounding. Then find the exact difference.

21. $65 - 42 =$

22. $431 - 297 =$

23. $852 - 361 =$

24. $631 - 288 =$

25. $1,961 - 457 =$

Multiplying Whole Numbers

EXAMPLE   Sometimes when multiplying, you will need to rename.
When a letter is part of the answer, remember to include it in the answer.

$$
\begin{array}{r}
2 \\
27a \\
\times\ 64 \\
\hline
108
\end{array}
\qquad
\begin{array}{r}
4 \\
27a \\
\times\ 64 \\
\hline
108 \\
1{,}620
\end{array}
\qquad
\begin{array}{r}
27a \\
\times\ 64 \\
\hline
108 \\
1{,}620 \\
\hline
1{,}728a
\end{array}
$$

Multiply ones.   Multiply tens.   Add.
Rename.   Rename.

Directions Multiply the following problems.

1. $4 \times 8 =$ _____

2. $(7)(9) =$ _____

3. $9 \cdot 9 =$ _____

4. $5a \cdot 6 =$ _____

5. $(4)(3b) =$ _____

6. $10y \times 4 =$ _____

Directions Multiply. Remember to rename.

7.
$$
\begin{array}{r}
16 \\
\times\ 24 \\
\hline
\end{array}
$$

9.
$$
\begin{array}{r}
35x \\
\times\ 17 \\
\hline
\end{array}
$$

11.
$$
\begin{array}{r}
87z \\
\times\ 9 \\
\hline
\end{array}
$$

8.
$$
\begin{array}{r}
34 \\
\times\ 23 \\
\hline
\end{array}
$$

10.
$$
\begin{array}{r}
91 \\
\times\ 8x \\
\hline
\end{array}
$$

12.
$$
\begin{array}{r}
19c \\
\times\ 8 \\
\hline
\end{array}
$$

Directions Write each problem in vertical form. Then multiply.

13. $28 \times 76y$

14. $19 \times 32z$

15. $81b \times 22$

Dividing Whole Numbers

EXAMPLE   When dividing, place the numbers correctly in each step.

To check an answer, use multiplication and add the remainder.

Check

$$\begin{array}{r} 59\ r1 \\ 8\overline{)473} \\ \underline{40} \\ 73 \\ \underline{72} \\ 1 \end{array}$$

$8 \times 59 + 1 = 473$

Directions Divide these problems.

1. $45 \div 9 =$ _____

5. $36 \div 6 =$ _____

9. $10 \div 5 =$ _____

2. $16 \div 2 =$ _____

6. $9 \div 3 =$ _____

10. $33 \div 11 =$ _____

3. $27 \div 3 =$ _____

7. $18 \div 2 =$ _____

11. $48 \div 12 =$ _____

4. $14 \div 2 =$ _____

8. $72a \div 9 =$ _____

12. $54y \div 6 =$ _____

Directions Divide these problems.

13. $7\overline{)434}$

16. $8\overline{)272x}$

19. $9\overline{)463}$

14. $4\overline{)296}$

17. $3\overline{)402a}$

20. $2\overline{)365}$

15. $5\overline{)625}$

18. $6\overline{)528b}$

21. $8\overline{)682}$

Directions Divide. Check your work.

Check

Check

22. $18\overline{)4,482}$

24. $61\overline{)8,419}$

23. $27\overline{)2,457x}$

25. $43\overline{)5,762a}$

Basic Operations

EXAMPLE   There are four basic operations.

addition	$32 + 9 = 41$	multiplication	$8 \times 7 = 56$
subtraction	$44 - 20 = 24$	division	$36 \div 4 = 9$

Directions   Solve each problem.

1. $112a$
    $+ \ 9a$

6. 99
    $- \ 47$

11. $24\overline{)192a}$

2. $75\overline{)750}$

7. $74\overline{)2,368b}$

12. $48\overline{)96x}$

3. $16\overline{)224x}$

8. 639
    $+ \ 124$

13. $92x$
    $+ \ 12x$

4. 15
    $\times \ 15$

9. $34a$
    $\times \ 22$

14. $1,432b$
    $+ \ 3,698b$

5. $77a$
    $- \ 76a$

10. $36\overline{)936}$

15. 198
    $- \ 163$

Directions   Use a calculator to solve each problem.

16. $112,342 - 9,479 =$

18. $206 \cdot 432 =$

20. $114,204 \div 62 =$

_____

_____

_____

17. $6,048 \div 72 =$

19. $1,210 + 6,352 + 4,418 =$

_____

_____

Estimating Products and Quotients

EXAMPLE	To estimate a product, round to the greatest place value. Round up if 5 or more. Round down if less than 5.	To estimate a quotient, use two numbers that form a basic division fact.

$23 \times 67 =$

estimate $20 \times 70 = 1,400$

$1,721 \div 61 =$

$17 \div 6$ is not a basic fact.

$18 \div 6$ is a basic fact.

estimate $1,800 \div 60 = 30$

Directions Round. Estimate. Then find the exact product.

Problem	Rounded	Estimate	Exact Product
1. 63×24	_____	_____	_____
2. 85×36	_____	_____	_____
3. 17×42	_____	_____	_____
4. 44×75	_____	_____	_____
5. 59×14	_____	_____	_____
6. 32×55	_____	_____	_____
7. 73×64	_____	_____	_____
8. 27×83	_____	_____	_____

Directions Round. Estimate. Then find the exact quotient.

Problem	Rounded	Estimate	Exact Quotient
9. $534 \div 6$	_____	_____	_____
10. $736 \div 8$	_____	_____	_____
11. $1,380 \div 23$	_____	_____	_____
12. $2,862 \div 54$	_____	_____	_____
13. $6,290 \div 74$	_____	_____	_____
14. $4,758 \div 78$	_____	_____	_____
15. $11,613 \div 49$	_____	_____	_____

Open Statements

EXAMPLE

Four Basic Operations		True, False, and Open Statements	
addition	$21 + 7 = 28$	True	$31 + 4 = 35$
subtraction	$16 - 4 = 12$	False	$27 - 4 = 12$
multiplication	$8 \times 3 = 24$	Open	$45 + n = 51$
division	$18 \div 9 = 2$		

Directions Write the operation or operations used in each expression.

1. $6 + n$ _____

2. $48 \div b$ _____

3. $3x$ _____

4. $27 - y$ _____

5. $54n \div 9$ _____

6. $16 \cdot 18$ _____

7. $3\overline{)27}$ _____

8. $3x - 15$ _____

9. $74 + 6n$ _____

10. $6x + 17 - 8$ _____

Directions Write *true* if the statement is true or *false* if it is false. Write *open* if the statement is neither true nor false.

11. $13 + 8 = 21$ _____

12. $48 - 12 = 36$ _____

13. $6 \times 9 = 48$ _____

14. $42 \div 7 = 7$ _____

15. $83 + n = 92$ _____

16. $5 \cdot 4 = 20$ _____

17. $21 \div 7 = 3$ _____

18. $16 - b = 12$ _____

19. $15 \div 4 = 5$ _____

20. $126 + 10 = 116$ _____

21. $6n = 36$ _____

22. $12 \cdot 3 = 30$ _____

23. $n + 18 = 25$ _____

24. $64 - 23 = 41$ _____

25. $12n = 144$ _____

26. $66 \div 11 = 6$ _____

27. $16 - 6 = 20$ _____

28. $75 + 15 = 90$ _____

29. $n \div 8 = 2$ _____

30. $6 \times 7 = 42$ _____

Using Letters to Represent Numbers

EXAMPLE   Numerical Expressions (only numbers are used)

    $42 - 12$ 3×3

Algebraic Expressions (numbers and letters are used)

    $2x + 6$ $7a \div 3$

Variables (letters) n in $7n + 4$

Operations (addition, subtraction, multiplication, division)

    $6x + 4$ (multiplication and addition)

    $(18 \div 3) - 8$ (division and subtraction)

Directions Write *numerical* or *algebraic* for each expression.

1. $6x + 3$ _____

2. $24 - 16$ _____

3. $55 \div 11$ _____

4. $9x + 17$ _____

5. $128 + 76$ _____

6. $n + 19$ _____

7. $64 \div 8 - 7$ _____

8. 63×8 _____

9. $8b + 7b$ _____

10. $17c \div 3$ _____

Directions Identify the variable in each expression.

11. $6x + 17$ _____

12. $8 \div 2b$ _____

13. $16y - 8$ _____

14. $k + 12$ _____

15. $d \div 4$ _____

16. $x - 83$ _____

17. $4 + y$ _____

18. $3m \div 5$ _____

19. $4x + 12$ _____

20. $5d$ _____

Directions List the operation or operations used in each expression.

21. $8y - 16$ _____

22. 16×32 _____

23. $32 + 6b$ _____

24. $9 \cdot 17$ _____

25. $(16 \div 8) - y$ _____

Replacing Variables

EXAMPLE   This is how to evaluate whether an open statement is true or false.

Step 1 Substitute a number for the variable.

$6 + x = 11$ when $x = 5$
$6 + 5 = \square$

$8 - a = 6$ when $a = 3$
$8 - 3 = \square$

Step 2 Perform the operation.

$6 + 5 = 11$ is a true statement
$8 - 3 = 6$ is a false statement

Directions   Read each statement. Substitute each given number for n.
Write whether the statement is *true* or *false* for the value of n.

Statement: $6n = 30$

1. $n = 3$ _____

2. $n = 6$ _____

3. $n = 5$ _____

Statement: $21 + n = 28$

7. $n = 4$ _____

8. $n = 16$ _____

9. $n = 7$ _____

Statement: $12 - n = 7$

4. $n = 10$ _____

5. $n = 5$ _____

6. $n = 7$ _____

Statement: $36 \div n = 4$

10. $n = 9$ _____

11. $n = 6$ _____

12. $n = 5$ _____

Directions   Evaluate each expression.

13. $m + 17$ when m is 15 _____

14. $3x - 6$ when x is 3 _____

15. $18 \div g$ when g is 6 _____

16. $21 + 2c$ when c is 5 _____

17. $48 - g$ when g is 17 _____

18. $n \div 4$ when n is 24 _____

19. $8x$ when x is 8 _____

20. $27 - 3y$ when y is 3 _____

Place Value and Decimals

EXAMPLE

165.8742   The digit 1 is in the hundreds place.

The digit 6 is in the tens place.

The digit 5 is in the ones place.

The digit 8 is in the tenths place.

The digit 7 is in the hundredths place.

The digit 4 is in the thousandths place.

The digit 2 is in the ten-thousandths place.

The value of the digit 6 is 60. The value of the digit 7 is 0.07.

0.7 = seven tenths   0.42 = forty-two hundredths

Directions Write each number in words.

1. 0.3 _____

2. 0.81 _____

3. 0.12 _____

4. 0.077 _____

5. 0.325 _____

Directions Write the number expressed by each phrase.

6. forty-two one-hundredths

_____

7. seven tenths

_____

8. two one-hundredths

_____

9. thirty-three one-thousandths

_____

10. twenty-five one-hundredths

_____

Comparing and Rounding Decimals

EXAMPLE

Round 4.26 to the nearest tenth: 4.3

Round 8.241 to the nearest hundredth: 8.24

Round 2.7835 to the nearest thousandth: 2.784

Compare 6.8621 and 6.86.

Add two zeros to 6.86: 6.8600

6.8621 > 6.8600   6.8621 > 6.86

Directions Round each decimal to the nearest tenth.

1. 46.87 _____   **4.** 2.098 _____

2. 108.21 _____   **5.** 39.03 _____

3. 16.967 _____

Directions Round each decimal to the nearest hundredth.

6. 199.987 _____   **9.** 77.8061 _____

7. 20.062 _____   **10.** 10.7777 _____

8. 5.9927 _____

Directions Round each decimal to the nearest thousandth.

11. 13.4259 _____   **14.** 12.6669 _____

12. 0.0571 _____   **15.** 251.7032 _____

13. 399.1129 _____

Directions Compare each pair of decimals. Write < or >.

16. 17.092 ☐ 17.09 _____   **21.** 25.77 ☐ 25.771 _____

17. 2.3 ☐ 2.31 _____   **22.** 0.8871 ☐ 0.88711 _____

18. 937.328 ☐ 937.32 _____   **23.** 33.99 ☐ 33.909 _____

19. 14.8276 ☐ 14.82 _____   **24.** 406.22 ☐ 406.222 _____

20. 8.901 ☐ 8.9017 _____   **25.** 7.63954 ☐ 7.639549 _____

Adding and Subtracting Decimals

EXAMPLE

To find the perimeter of a triangle, use the formula $P = a + b + c$
where a, b, and c are the lengths of the sides of the triangle.

Triangle A: $a = 4.23$ cm $b = 13.1$ cm $c = 10.012$ cm

To add or subtract decimals, add zeros where necessary and line up the decimal points.

```
   4.230
  13.100
+ 10.012
  27.342 cm
```

Directions The numbers below show the length of each side of a triangle. Find the perimeter of each triangle.

1. 3.42 cm, 8.19 cm, 4.5 cm _____

2. 0.663 cm, 1.12 cm, 0.997 cm _____

3. 18.02 cm, 16.477 cm, 13.9 cm _____

4. 1.7 cm, 2.34 cm, 2.11 cm _____

5. 8.176 cm, 12.5 cm, 10.015 cm _____

6. 13.459 cm, 17.847 cm, 19.003 cm _____

7. 29.317 cm, 33.822 cm, 21.1 cm _____

8. 0.168 cm, 3.04 cm, 2.3 cm _____

9. 7.65 cm, 6.011 cm, 9.7 cm _____

Directions Add or subtract the dollar amounts.

10. $39.75 – $18.98 _____

11. $0.84 – $0.67 _____

12. $494.16 + $78.87 _____

13. $100.00 – $16.29 _____

14. $1.45 – $0.76 _____

15. $991.81 – $4.92 _____

16. $323.13 + $9.99 _____

17. $17.32 – $0.54 _____

Directions Solve the problems.

18. Jon and Brooke each planted a bean seed. Jon's plant grew to 9.967 cm. Brooke's plant grew to 13.14 cm. How much taller was Brooke's plant than Jon's? _____

19. Alana earned $9.75 selling vegetables from her garden in June, $62 in July, and $109.25 in August. What were Alana's total earnings from her garden for the three months? _____

20. Julio rode his bicycle 32.097 miles on Saturday and 9.84 miles on Sunday. How many more miles did he ride on Saturday than on Sunday? _____

Multiplying Decimals by Powers of 10

EXAMPLE

$10^2 = 100$ $10^3 = 1,000$ $10^4 = 10,000$

$8.52 \times 100 = 852$

Move the decimal point two places to the right.

$5.37 \times 10^3 = 5,370$

Move the decimal point three places to the right.

Directions   Rewrite each operation by replacing the power of 10 with its equivalent number. Then multiply.

45.6×10^3	$45.6 \times 1,000$	$45,600$
2.345×10^1	**1.** _____	**2.** _____
17.425×10^2	**3.** _____	**4.** _____
8.7×10^4	**5.** _____	**6.** _____
0.0651×10^5	**7.** _____	**8.** _____
643×10^2	**9.** _____	**10.** _____

Directions   Rewrite each operation by writing the multiple of 10 as a power of 10. Then multiply.

12.8×100	12.8×10^2	$1,280$
$0.53219 \times 1,000$	**11.** _____	**12.** _____
44.22×10	**13.** _____	**14.** _____
$1.359 \times 10,000$	**15.** _____	**16.** _____
$39.71 \times 100,000$	**17.** _____	**18.** _____
0.07125×100	**19.** _____	**20.** _____

Name_____ Date_____ Period_____

Multiplying Decimals

EXAMPLE To find the circumference of a circle, use the formula $C = \pi d$.

C = circumference π = pi (about 3.14)   d = diameter

Find the circumference of a circle with a diameter of 4.3 cm.

$C = \pi \times 4.3$

$C = 3.14 \times 4.3$

```
    3.14
 ×   4.3
    942
  1256
  13.502
```

$C = 13.502$ cm

Directions Find the circumference of each circle with the diameter shown.
You may use your calculator.

1. $d = 7.2$ cm _____

2. $d = 2.9$ inches _____

3. $d = 14$ cm _____

4. $d = 18.12$ cm _____

5. $d = 5.67$ inches _____

6. $d = 0.53$ inches _____

7. $d = 64.3$ cm _____

8. $d = 29.1$ inches _____

9. $d = 13.37$ cm _____

10. $d = 3.693$ cm _____

Directions Multiply.

11. 4.36×7 _____

12. 9.11×4 _____

13. 5.46×3 _____

14. 12.07×3.2 _____

15. 2.8×7.1 _____

16. 8.13×23.22 _____

17. 90.17×3.21 _____

18. 4.305×0.216 _____

19. 77.12×9.332 _____

20. 81.51×3.67 _____

Dividing Decimals by Powers of 10

EXAMPLE

$2.6 \div 100 = 0.026$

Move the decimal point two places to the left.

$643.50 \div 1,000 = 0.6435$

Move the decimal point three places to the left.

Directions   Complete the chart by dividing each number by the power of 10 shown.

	10^1	10^2	10^3	10^4
824.2	82.42	**1.**	0.8242	**2.**
61.49	**3.**	**4.**	**5.**	**6.**
0.267	**7.**	**8.**	**9.**	**10.**
3.195	**11.**	**12.**	**13.**	**14.**
0.53	**15.**	**16.**	**17.**	**18.**
184.75	**19.**	**20.**	**21.**	**22.**
7.08	**23.**	**24.**	**25.**	**26.**
14.85	**27.**	**28.**	**29.**	**30.**

Dividing Decimals

EXAMPLE

$$
\begin{array}{r}
3.68 \\
5\overline{)18.40} \\
-15 \\
\hline
34 \\
-30 \\
\hline
40 \\
-40 \\
\hline
0
\end{array}
$$

$$1.5\overline{)9.75}$$

$$
\begin{array}{r}
6.5 \\
15\overline{)97.5} \\
-90 \\
\hline
75 \\
-75 \\
\hline
0
\end{array}
$$

Directions Divide.

1. $18.76 \div 4$ _____

2. $78.84 \div 8$ _____

3. $48.96 \div 3$ _____

4. $18.84 \div 12$ _____

5. $28.71 \div 9$ _____

6. $59.90 \div 5$ _____

7. $121.28 \div 32$ _____

8. $223.14 \div 6$ _____

9. $154.62 \div 9$ _____

10. $119.32 \div 4$ _____

Directions Divide. Round your answer to the nearest hundredth. You may use your calculator.

11. $58.86 \div 0.6$ _____

12. $4.851 \div 0.3$ _____

13. $137.28 \div 5.2$ _____

14. $35.87 \div 1.74$ _____

15. $155.52 \div 8.1$ _____

16. $728.52 \div 1.2$ _____

17. $34.84 \div 0.04$ _____

18. $0.8665 \div 0.05$ _____

19. $75.12 \div 0.823$ _____

20. $385.14 \div 2.1$ _____

Using Decimals

1. Luis brought 12 pounds of aluminum cans to the recycling center. He received $3.36. How much does the recycling center pay for each pound of aluminum? _____

2. The average temperature in Key West, Florida, is 77.7°F. The average temperature in International Falls, Minnesota, is 36.4°F. On average, how much warmer is it in Key West than in International Falls? _____

3. A small swimming pool holds 5,263 gallons of water. A bathtub holds 55.4 gallons of water. How many times would you have to fill the bathtub to use the amount of water it takes to fill the pool? _____

4. Sam earned $5.75 for mowing the lawn, $14.50 for delivering newspapers, and $12.00 for washing windows last week. How much did he earn? _____

5. The George Washington Bridge is 1,066.8 m long. The Golden Gate Bridge is 213.4 m longer than the George Washington Bridge. How long is the Golden Gate Bridge? _____

6. Gina rode 496.24 miles on a bicycle trip. The trip took 9 days. What was the average number of miles Gina rode each day? Round your answer to the nearest tenth. _____

7. A recipe for fruit salad calls for 1.5 pounds of apples, 2 pounds of oranges, and 1.25 pounds of grapes. At the market, apples cost $0.69 per pound, oranges cost $0.79 per pound, and grapes cost $0.86 per pound. How much will it cost to make the fruit salad? _____

8. Jim's grandparents sent him $35.00 for his birthday. He bought a CD for $12.99 and put $15.00 in his savings account. How much did Jim have left? _____

9. Kay purchased 16 tomato plants for $0.48 each. How much did she spend? _____

10. A camper hiked 41.7 kilometers on the first day, 21.2 kilometers on the second day, and 37.4 kilometers on the third day. How many more kilometers did the camper hike on the first two days than on the third day? _____

Decimals and Fractions

EXAMPLE

Write 0.25 as a fraction.   5 is in the hundredths place. The denominator is 100.

$\frac{25}{100} = \frac{1}{4}$

Write $\frac{29}{100}$ as a decimal.   0.29

Write $\frac{30}{50}$ as a decimal. $\frac{30}{50} = \frac{30 \times 2}{50 \times 2} = \frac{60}{100}$ $\frac{60}{100} = 0.60$

Directions Write the denominator that would be used to change each decimal to a fraction.

1. 0.7 _____

2. 0.21 _____

3. 0.03 _____

4. 0.1 _____

5. 0.119 _____

Directions Write each decimal as a fraction. Simplify.

6. 0.34 _____

7. 0.24 _____

8. 0.45 _____

9. 0.010 _____

10. 0.2 _____

11. 0.13 _____

12. 3.08 _____

13. 0.006 _____

14. 0.36 _____

15. 7.8 _____

Directions Write each fraction as a decimal.

16. $\frac{8}{25}$ _____

17. $\frac{3}{20}$ _____

18. $1\frac{7}{50}$ _____

19. $\frac{29}{40}$ _____

20. $\frac{13}{20}$ _____

21. $3\frac{18}{25}$ _____

22. $\frac{3}{8}$ _____

23. $7\frac{1}{5}$ _____

24. $\frac{61}{100}$ _____

25. $\frac{16}{25}$ _____

Repeating Decimals

EXAMPLE   To change degrees Fahrenheit to degrees Celsius, use the formula $C = \frac{5}{9}(F - 32)$.

45 degrees F = how many degrees Celsius?

$C = \frac{5}{9}(45 - 32)$

$C = \frac{5}{9}(13)$

$C = \frac{65}{9}$

$C = 7.2222$ To write a repeating decimal, write a bar over the repeating digits.

$7.\overline{2}$

You may round off a temperature to the nearest degree: 7°C

Directions   Find the Celsius temperature for each Fahrenheit temperature.
Round each answer to the nearest whole degree.

1. F = 24°   _____

2. F = 109°   _____

3. F = 84°   _____

4. F = 68°   _____

5. F = 32°   _____

6. F = 76°   _____

7. F = 42°   _____

8. F = 164°   _____

9. F = 52°   _____

10. F = 90°   _____

Directions   Write each fraction as a repeating decimal.

11. $\frac{2}{9}$ _____

12. $\frac{8}{15}$ _____

13. $\frac{5}{9}$ _____

14. $\frac{1}{6}$ _____

15. $\frac{4}{15}$ _____

16. $\frac{7}{9}$ _____

17. $\frac{3}{11}$ _____

18. $\frac{7}{12}$ _____

19. $\frac{13}{18}$ _____

20. $\frac{2}{11}$ _____

Renaming Percents to Decimals

EXAMPLE

5% = 0.05

$8\frac{1}{2}\% = .085$

What is the interest for one year on a principal of $600 at a rate of 7%?

$I = p \times r \times t$

$I = 600 \times 0.07 \times 1$

$I = \$42.00$

Directions Change each percent to a decimal.

1. 18% _____

2. 94% _____

3. 0.3% _____

4. $2\frac{3}{4}\%$ _____

5. 29% _____

6. 300% _____

7. 48% _____

8. 1.2% _____

9. 81% _____

10. 2% _____

Directions Find the interest each principal will earn. If necessary, round each answer to the nearest cent.

11. Principal: $18,500
Rate: 9.75%
Time: 9 months

_____

12. Principal: $750
Rate: 6.75%
Time: 6 months

_____

13. Principal: $1,200
Rate: 5.75%
Time: 1 year

_____

14. Principal: $6,400
Rate: 5%
Time: 2 years

_____

15. Principal: $11,650
Rate: 7%
Time: 3 months

_____

Evaluating Expressions with Decimals

EXAMPLE

Evaluate 6.21*n* when *n* = 3.2

6.21 × 3.2 = 19.872

Directions Evaluate each expression.

1. $p - 8.02$ when $p = 62.35$ _____

2. $n + 14.375$ when $n = 0.027$ _____

3. $s \div 0.125$ when $s = 3$ _____

4. $73.21a$ when $a = 1.19$ _____

5. $9p + 16n$ when $p = 7.26$ and $n = 0.24$ _____

Directions Solve each problem.

6. Lucia has *n* dollars. Kelly has $12.81 more than Lucia. Write an algebraic expression for how much money Kelly has. Then evaluate the expression when *n* = $37.65. _____

_____

7. Fox Hills has *l* number of lots with 4.2 acres in each lot. Forest Point has *m* number of lots with 5.6 acres in each lot. Write an algebraic expression showing how many acres are in Fox Hills and Forest Point combined. Then evaluate the expression when *l* = 13 and *m* = 8. _____

_____

8. Anthony has *p* dollars in his bank account. He spends $42.95 on a sweater. Write an algebraic expression for how much Anthony will have left in the bank after he buys the sweater. Then evaluate the expression when *p* = $116.80. _____

_____

9. Jim has *n* number of employees. His payroll totals $4,503.04 per week. Write an algebraic expression for how much each employee is paid per week if all employees receive equal pay. Then evaluate the expression when *n* = 8. _____

_____

10. Martina sold *l* number of paintings. Each painting cost $125.75. Write an algebraic expression for the total amount Martina made on her paintings. Then evaluate the expression when *l* = 18. _____

_____

Divisibility Rules

EXAMPLE

A number that can be divided by a whole number with no remainder is said to be divisible.

The symbol | means divides.

2|10 is a true statement because 10 is divisible by 2 and there is no remainder.
     10 ÷ 2 = 5 (no remainder)

2|17 is a false statement because 17 is not divisible by 2 without leaving a remainder.
     17 ÷ 2 = 8 r1

Directions Write *true* if the statement is true and *false* if the statement is
false. Write a division equation to prove your answer.

1. 5|15   _____   _____

2. 4|36   _____   _____

3. 6|39   _____   _____

4. 8|40   _____   _____

5. 9|82   _____   _____

6. 6|46   _____   _____

7. 3|90   _____   _____

8. 5|85   _____   _____

9. 4|128   _____   _____

10. 8|374   _____   _____

11. 2|577   _____   _____

12. 4|634   _____   _____

13. 9|567   _____   _____

14. 7|473   _____   _____

15. 8|688   _____   _____

Prime and Composite Numbers

EXAMPLE   A prime number has two factors: 1 and itself.

5 is a prime number. Its factors are 5 and 1. $5 \times 1 = 5$

A composite number has factors other than 1 and itself.

14 is a composite number. Its two factors are 7 and 2. $7 \times 2 = 14$

Directions   Write the numbers in each pair in the correct column to show which number is a prime number and which number is a composite number.

	Prime	Composite
1. 3, 6		
2. 8, 17		
3. 27, 31		
4. 5, 12		
5. 13, 16		
6. 43, 50		
7. 20, 41		
8. 83, 106		
9. 125, 149		
10. 97, 221		

	Prime	Composite
11. 7, 12		
12. 20, 37		
13. 38, 41		
14. 81, 89		
15. 67, 121		
16. 72, 79		
17. 177, 691		
18. 197, 221		
19. 109, 301		
20. 108, 239		

Directions   Circle two factors for each composite number.

21. 18	2	5	8	9		**26.** 35	4	5	6	7
22. 21	3	5	7	8		**27.** 48	5	6	8	9
23. 15	3	4	5	6		**28.** 45	2	4	5	9
24. 24	4	5	6	9		**29.** 12	3	4	5	7
25. 32	3	4	6	8		**30.** 30	4	5	6	8

Greatest Common Divisor

EXAMPLE

To find the greatest common divisor (GCD) of two numbers, list all the factors.
The greatest common factor is the greatest common divisor.

(14, 21) 14:   1   2   ⑦   14

          21:    1   3   ⑦   21

7 is the greatest common divisor (GCD) of 14 and 21.

Directions Write the factors for each number. Then write the greatest common divisor (GCD).

Factors

GCD

1. (9, 24)   9: _____

                   24: _____   _____

2. (14, 28)   14: _____

                   28: _____   _____

3. (8, 16)   8: _____

                   16: _____   _____

4. (11, 77)   11: _____

                   77: _____   _____

5. (4, 20)   4: _____

                   20: _____   _____

6. (3x, 21)   3x: _____

                   21: _____   _____

7. (8, 48y)   8: _____

                   48y: _____   _____

8. (12x, 60x) 12x: _____

                   60x: _____   _____

9. (7a, 42a)   7a: _____

                   42a: _____   _____

10. (6c, 54c) 6c: _____

                   54c: _____   _____

Factoring

EXAMPLE

Factor $6x + 8$.

Step 1 Find the greatest common divisor.

| $6x$: | 1 | ② | 3 | 6 | x |
| 8: | 1 | ② | 4 | 8 |

Step 2 Write the GCD outside parentheses. $2(\quad)$

Step 3 Use the distributive property in reverse. $2(3x + 4)$

Step 4 Check using the distributive property.

$2(3x + 4) = (2 \cdot 3x) + (2 \cdot 4) = 6x + 8$

Directions Circle the GCD for each expression.

1. $3x + 9$	1	3	9		**6.** $30y + 36z$	3	5	6
2. $12y + 18$	2	3	6		**7.** $9d + 54e$	3	6	9
3. $32b + 8$	4	8	16		**8.** $3c + 7y$	1	3	7
4. $44a + 4$	2	4	11		**9.** $25d + 100c$	4	5	25
5. $10z + 50b$	2	5	10		**10.** $18x + 33y$	3	6	11

Directions Use the distributive property to factor each expression.

11. $18x + 12$ _____

12. $6y + 8$ _____

13. $3c + 9$ _____

14. $6a + 15$ _____

15. $2h + 11$ _____

16. $54b + 9w$ _____

17. $20m + 15k$ _____

18. $12n + 4p$ _____

19. $9q + 81c$ _____

20. $ab + bc$ _____

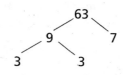
Least Common Multiple

EXAMPLE   Find the least common multiple (LCM) of 48 and 63.

Step 1 Write the prime factorization of each number.

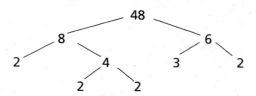

2 • 2 • 2 • 2 • 3 or 2^4 • 3
(prime factorization)

3 • 3 • 7 or 3^2 • 7
(prime factorization)

Step 2 Identify the greatest power of each prime factor.
The greatest power of the prime factor 2 is 2^4.
The greatest power of the prime factor 3 is 3^2.
The greatest power of the prime factor 7 is 7.

Step 3 Find the product.
2^4 • 3^2 • 7 = 16 • 9 • 7 = 1,008

The LCM of 48 and 63 is 1,008.

Directions Complete each factor tree.

1. 72

2. 27

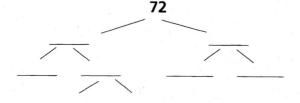

Directions Write the prime factorization for each factor tree above.

3. _____

4. _____

Directions Find each least common multiple (LCM).

5. LCM (4, 12) _____

6. LCM (5, 18) _____

7. LCM (30, 60) _____

8. LCM (16, 35) _____

9. LCM (10, 28) _____

10. LCM (21, 24) _____

Scientific Notation

EXAMPLE

To write large numbers using scientific notation, move the decimal to make a number between 1 and 10.

Count the number of places the decimal was moved.

$65,000,000 = 6.5 \times 10^7$

7 654 321 (number of places from the decimal point = 7)

$0.658 = 6.58 \times 10^{-1}$ (number of places from the decimal point = 1)

If the decimal is moved to the left, the exponent is positive. (10^7)

If the decimal is moved to the right, the exponent is negative. (10^{-1})

Directions To write the number in scientific notation: Write how many places each decimal must be moved. Write *left* or *right* to tell in which direction to move the decimal point.

Number	Places Moved	Direction	Scientific Notation
1. 325,000	_____	_____	_____
2. 27,800	_____	_____	_____
3. 105,000,000	_____	_____	_____
4. 0.653	_____	_____	_____
5. 0.0325	_____	_____	_____
6. 0.0000817	_____	_____	_____
7. 681,000,000,000	_____	_____	_____
8. 0.000000783	_____	_____	_____
9. 0.00001818	_____	_____	_____
10. 86,000,000,000	_____	_____	_____

Directions Write the number that each example of scientific notation stands for.

11. 6.2×10^2 _____

12. 8.7×10^4 _____

13. 3.87×10^8 _____

14. 7.15×10^{-1} _____

15. 3.84×10^{-2} _____

Name _____   Date _____   Period _____

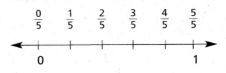

Proper Fractions

EXAMPLE   Which proper fractions are named by this number line?

Step 1   Count the total number of marks between 0 and 1, including the mark at 1. This will tell you the denominator.

Step 2   Counting each mark away from 0 will tell you the numerator.

The following are proper fractions: $\frac{0}{5}$ $\frac{1}{5}$ $\frac{2}{5}$ $\frac{3}{5}$ $\frac{4}{5}$.

Directions   Write the proper fraction that represents the shaded part of each whole or set.

1.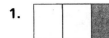

2.   ● ○ ○ ○ ● ○ ● ○

3.   ▷ ▷ ▶ ▶ ▷

_____   _____   _____

Directions   Which proper fractions are named by these number lines?

4.

5.

6.

_____   _____   _____

Directions   Write a proper fraction to answer each question.

7. Julie has 15 new pencils. Eleven of them are primary colors. What part of the total number of pencils are primary colors?   _____

8. Ed took a survey of students in his math class. Fifteen out of a total of 21 students have pets. What part of the total number of students have pets?   _____

9. Twenty-three students in Mrs. Edwards' music class were also taking Spanish. Mrs. Edwards has a total of 27 students. What part of the total class was taking Spanish?   _____

10. Isaac checked out eight books from the library. He read only three of them before he had to return them. What part of the whole number of books did he read?   _____

Improper Fractions and Mixed Numbers

EXAMPLE Express $\frac{11}{3}$ as a mixed number.

$$\frac{11}{3} = 11 \div 3 = 3\overline{)11}^{\,3}$$
$$\underline{-9}$$
$$2 \quad \text{Write the remainder as a fraction: } \frac{11}{3} = 3\frac{2}{3}$$

Directions Express each improper fraction as a mixed or whole number.

1. $\frac{8}{3}$ _____

2. $\frac{9}{5}$ _____

3. $\frac{10}{2}$ _____

4. $\frac{21}{6}$ _____

5. $\frac{11}{8}$ _____

6. $\frac{25}{8}$ _____

7. $\frac{32}{5}$ _____

8. $\frac{12}{11}$ _____

9. $\frac{36}{6}$ _____

10. $\frac{32}{10}$ _____

11. $\frac{15}{4}$ _____

12. $\frac{7}{7}$ _____

13. $\frac{9}{2}$ _____

14. $\frac{26}{19}$ _____

15. $\frac{8}{7}$ _____

Directions Express each number as an improper fraction.

16. $4\frac{2}{3}$ _____

17. $2\frac{5}{8}$ _____

18. $5\frac{1}{3}$ _____

19. $1\frac{9}{11}$ _____

20. $4\frac{2}{7}$ _____

21. $68\frac{1}{3}$ _____

22. $12\frac{1}{2}$ _____

23. $7\frac{7}{8}$ _____

24. $12\frac{3}{4}$ _____

25. $7\frac{1}{2}$ _____

26. $9\frac{3}{4}$ _____

27. $33\frac{1}{2}$ _____

28. $14\frac{1}{5}$ _____

29. $9\frac{9}{10}$ _____

30. $18\frac{4}{5}$ _____

Equivalent Fractions

EXAMPLE   Write an equivalent fraction for $\frac{2}{5}$.

Multiply the numerator and the denominator of $\frac{2}{5}$ by 3.

$$\frac{2}{5} \cdot \frac{3}{3} = \frac{6}{15}$$

Directions Write two equivalent fractions for each fraction.

1. $\frac{2}{3}$ _____

2. $\frac{3}{4}$ _____

3. $\frac{5}{6}$ _____

4. $\frac{1}{16}$ _____

5. $\frac{2}{5}$ _____

6. $\frac{7}{10}$ _____

7. $\frac{2}{7}$ _____

8. $\frac{5}{9}$ _____

9. $\frac{1}{2}$ _____

10. $\frac{3}{10}$ _____

EXAMPLE   Use a calculator to decide if $\frac{3}{8}$ and $\frac{9}{24}$ are equal.

For $\frac{3}{8}$: Press 3 ⌈÷⌋ 8 ⌈=⌋. The display reads 0.375.

For $\frac{9}{24}$: Press 9 ⌈÷⌋ 24 ⌈=⌋. The display reads 0.375.

Since the answers are the same, the fractions are equal.
If the answers are not the same, the fractions are not equivalent.

Directions Use your calculator to decide if the two fractions are equivalent.
Write *yes* or *no*.

11. $\frac{1}{2}$ and $\frac{15}{30}$ _____

12. $\frac{16}{35}$ and $\frac{8}{17}$ _____

13. $\frac{11}{12}$ and $\frac{33}{40}$ _____

14. $\frac{4}{20}$ and $\frac{1}{4}$ _____

15. $\frac{6}{7}$ and $\frac{30}{35}$ _____

16. $\frac{20}{55}$ and $\frac{2}{5}$ _____

17. $\frac{4}{5}$ and $\frac{8}{10}$ _____

18. $\frac{3}{4}$ and $\frac{2}{3}$ _____

19. $\frac{7}{8}$ and $\frac{28}{32}$ _____

20. $\frac{15}{30}$ and $\frac{5}{10}$ _____

21. $\frac{9}{15}$ and $\frac{6}{8}$ _____

22. $\frac{3}{21}$ and $\frac{2}{14}$ _____

23. $\frac{20}{30}$ and $\frac{4}{6}$ _____

24. $\frac{6}{12}$ and $\frac{9}{20}$ _____

25. $\frac{5}{8}$ and $\frac{15}{16}$ _____

Simplest Form

EXAMPLE   Find GCD (10, 15).

List all of the factors of each number and circle the common factors.

10: ①   2   ⑤   10

15: ①   3   ⑤   15

Choose the *greatest* common factor.   GCD (10, 15) = 5

Directions Find the greatest common divisor (GCD) of each pair of numbers.

1. $(8, 24)$ _____

2. $(5, 10)$ _____

3. $(14, 16)$ _____

4. $(9, 12)$ _____

5. $(8, 10)$ _____

Directions Express each fraction in simplest form.

6. $\frac{10}{15}$ _____

7. $\frac{16}{24}$ _____

8. $\frac{78}{90}$ _____

9. $\frac{10}{50}$ _____

10. $\frac{55}{66}$ _____

11. $\frac{12}{15}$ _____

12. $\frac{8}{20}$ _____

13. $\frac{6}{9}$ _____

14. $\frac{18}{20}$ _____

15. $\frac{48}{60}$ _____

16. $\frac{20}{80}$ _____

17. $\frac{63}{108}$ _____

18. $\frac{27}{54}$ _____

19. $\frac{16}{48}$ _____

20. $\frac{81}{108}$ _____

21. $\frac{60}{90}$ _____

22. $\frac{30}{65}$ _____

Directions Solve the problems.

23. Shelly said she has $\frac{6}{8}$ of all the 1998 NFL collectors' cards. Mark said he has $\frac{9}{12}$ of them. Do they have the same number of cards? Explain.

_____

24. Ashley said $\frac{3}{4}$ of her stuffed animals have button eyes. Pam said Ashley has 15 stuffed animals. Is it possible that Pam is correct? Explain.

_____

25. Vince said his survey showed $\frac{2}{3}$ of his math class liked rap music. There are 24 students in the class. Is it possible that Vince's survey is correct? Explain.

_____

Comparing and Ordering Fractions

EXAMPLE Compare the fractions. Write > or <.

$$\frac{4}{5} \underline{\quad} \frac{3}{4}$$

Step 1 Write equivalent fractions using the LCM.

$$\frac{4}{5} = \frac{16}{20}$$

$$\frac{3}{4} = \frac{12}{20}$$

Step 2 Compare $\frac{16}{20}$ and $\frac{12}{20}$. $\frac{16}{20}$ is greater than $\frac{12}{20}$. $\frac{4}{5} > \frac{3}{4}$

Directions Compare the fractions. Write > or <.

1. $\frac{5}{8} \underline{\quad} \frac{1}{2}$

2. $\frac{8}{9} \underline{\quad} \frac{2}{3}$

3. $\frac{3}{4} \underline{\quad} \frac{4}{5}$

4. $\frac{4}{7} \underline{\quad} \frac{2}{5}$

5. $\frac{1}{5} \underline{\quad} \frac{1}{3}$

6. $\frac{6}{15} \underline{\quad} \frac{9}{15}$

7. $\frac{2}{3} \underline{\quad} \frac{5}{12}$

8. $\frac{3}{16} \underline{\quad} \frac{1}{4}$

9. $\frac{7}{8} \underline{\quad} \frac{3}{4}$

10. $4\frac{1}{2} \underline{\quad} 5\frac{2}{3}$

11. $6\frac{2}{5} \underline{\quad} 6\frac{3}{10}$

EXAMPLE Order $\frac{2}{3}$, $\frac{1}{2}$, and $\frac{3}{4}$ from least to greatest.

Step 1 Write equivalent fractions using the LCM.

$$\frac{2}{3} = \frac{8}{12} \qquad \frac{1}{2} = \frac{6}{12} \qquad \frac{3}{4} = \frac{9}{12}$$

Step 2 Compare $\frac{8}{12}$, $\frac{6}{12}$, and $\frac{9}{12}$. $\frac{6}{12} < \frac{8}{12} < \frac{9}{12}$

Therefore, the order from least to greatest is $\frac{1}{2}$, $\frac{2}{3}$, $\frac{3}{4}$.

Directions Order from least to greatest.

12. $\frac{2}{3}$ $\frac{3}{8}$ $\frac{1}{2}$ _____

13. $\frac{1}{2}$ $\frac{1}{3}$ $\frac{1}{4}$ _____

14. $\frac{3}{4}$ $\frac{3}{5}$ $\frac{2}{3}$ _____

15. $\frac{7}{8}$ $\frac{1}{2}$ $\frac{3}{4}$ _____

16. $\frac{3}{16}$ $\frac{7}{8}$ $\frac{2}{3}$ _____

17. $\frac{7}{10}$ $\frac{3}{5}$ $\frac{17}{20}$ _____

18. $\frac{5}{16}$ $\frac{9}{32}$ $\frac{1}{4}$ _____

19. $\frac{3}{35}$ $\frac{3}{7}$ $\frac{3}{5}$ _____

20. $\frac{3}{8}$ $\frac{5}{16}$ $\frac{1}{2}$ _____

Fractions—Like Denominators

EXAMPLE

Find $(1\frac{2}{3} + 2\frac{2}{3}) - 3\frac{1}{3}$

Step 1 Perform the computation inside the ( ) first.

$$(1\frac{2}{3} + 2\frac{2}{3}) - 3\frac{1}{3} =$$
$$4\frac{1}{3} \qquad - 3\frac{1}{3} =$$

Step 2 Perform the remaining computation.

$$4\frac{1}{3} - 3\frac{1}{3} = 1$$

Directions Add or subtract. If necessary, perform the computation inside the ( ) first. Write your answer in simplest form.

1. $\frac{3}{5} - \frac{2}{5}$ _____

2. $\frac{5}{6} + \frac{5}{6}$ _____

3. $\frac{9}{10} - \frac{7}{10}$ _____

4. $2\frac{15}{16} - 1\frac{7}{16}$ _____

5. $11\frac{11}{12} - 5\frac{9}{12}$ _____

6. $4\frac{3}{4} - 2\frac{1}{4}$ _____

7. $6\frac{7}{15} + 8\frac{14}{15}$ _____

8. $\frac{5x}{8} - \frac{3x}{8}$ _____

9. $\frac{9x}{10} - \frac{6x}{10}$ _____

10. $\frac{6}{y} + \frac{7}{y}$ _____

11. $\frac{4}{y} + \frac{x}{y}$ _____

12. $\frac{3x}{4} - \frac{x}{4}$ _____

13. $\frac{y}{16} + \frac{9y}{16}$ _____

14. $\frac{3y}{12} + \frac{5}{12}$ _____

15. $\frac{4x}{9} + \frac{10x}{9}$ _____

16. $(\frac{9}{10} + \frac{3}{10}) - \frac{4}{10}$ _____

17. $\frac{3}{8} + (\frac{7}{8} - \frac{4}{8})$ _____

18. $\frac{7}{16} - (\frac{1}{16} + \frac{3}{16})$ _____

19. $(\frac{8}{11} - \frac{5}{11}) + \frac{6}{11}$ _____

20. $\frac{11}{12} + (\frac{6}{12} - \frac{1}{12})$ _____

21. $\frac{4}{6} - (\frac{4}{6} - \frac{2}{6})$ _____

22. $\frac{3}{25} + (\frac{24}{25} - \frac{16}{25})$ _____

23. $(\frac{3x}{8} + \frac{9x}{8}) - \frac{5x}{8}$ _____

24. $\frac{2x}{3} + (\frac{2x}{3} - \frac{x}{3})$ _____

25. $\frac{3y}{12} + (\frac{9y}{12} - \frac{5y}{12})$ _____

Name _____ Date _____ Period _____

Fractions—Unlike Denominators

EXAMPLE Add $6\frac{2}{3} + 3\frac{1}{2}$.

Step 1 Find the LCM of the denominators.

LCM $(2, 3) = 6$

Step 2 Write an equivalent mixed number for each fraction using the LCM.

$\frac{2}{3} \cdot \frac{2}{2} = \frac{4}{6}$ $\qquad$ $6\frac{2}{3} = 6\frac{4}{6}$

$\frac{1}{2} \cdot \frac{3}{3} = \frac{3}{6}$ $\qquad$ $3\frac{1}{2} = 3\frac{3}{6}$

Step 3 Add. $\quad 6\frac{4}{6} + 3\frac{3}{6} = 9\frac{7}{6}$

Step 4 Simplify. $\qquad 9\frac{7}{6} = 10\frac{1}{6}$

Directions Add or subtract. Write your answer in simplest form.

1. $\frac{2}{3} + \frac{5}{6}$ _____

2. $\frac{7}{8} - \frac{7}{16}$ _____

3. $\frac{3}{4} + \frac{2}{3}$ _____

4. $\frac{9}{10} - \frac{3}{4}$ _____

5. $\frac{3}{5} - \frac{7}{45}$ _____

6. $\frac{19}{20} - \frac{3}{4}$ _____

7. $\frac{5}{8} + \frac{5}{6}$ _____

8. $\frac{4}{5} - \frac{2}{3}$ _____

9. $\frac{15}{16} + \frac{1}{2}$ _____

10. $\frac{11}{12} + \frac{3}{4}$ _____

Directions Add or subtract. Write your answer in simplest form.

11. $\frac{4x}{7} - \frac{x}{3}$ _____

12. $\frac{1}{x} + \frac{4}{y}$ _____

13. $\frac{5x}{12} + \frac{7x}{8}$ _____

14. $\frac{1}{2y} + \frac{5}{16y}$ _____

15. $\frac{3x}{4} - \frac{2x}{3}$ _____

Directions Add or subtract. Write your answer in simplest form.

16. $5\frac{7}{8} + 6\frac{3}{5}$ _____

17. $2\frac{3}{7} - 1\frac{1}{3}$ _____

18. $8\frac{9}{10} + 6\frac{1}{5}$ _____

19. $10\frac{3}{5} - 2\frac{3}{10}$ _____

20. $2\frac{7}{12} + 13\frac{3}{4}$ _____

21. $16\frac{5}{16} - 10\frac{7}{32}$ _____

22. $5\frac{5}{8} - 4\frac{2}{5}$ _____

23. $42\frac{5}{6} + 22\frac{7}{12}$ _____

24. $6\frac{3}{4}x + 2\frac{5}{8}x$ _____

25. $3\frac{4}{5}x - 2\frac{3}{10}x$ _____

Subtracting Fractions with Regrouping

EXAMPLE   Solve $4\frac{3}{8} - 2\frac{2}{3}$.

Step 1 Find the LCM of the denominators.
LCM (8, 3) = 24

Step 2 Write equivalent mixed numbers for $4\frac{3}{8}$ and $2\frac{2}{3}$ using the LCM (24) as denominators.

$$4\frac{3}{8} = 4\frac{9}{24} \qquad\qquad 2\frac{2}{3} = 2\frac{16}{24}$$

Step 3 Since $\frac{16}{24}$ cannot be subtracted from $\frac{9}{24}$, it must be renamed.

$$4\frac{9}{24} = 3\frac{33}{24} \qquad \text{(Think: } 4\frac{9}{24} = 3\frac{9}{24} + \frac{24}{24} = 3\frac{33}{24}\text{)}$$

Step 4 Subtract.

$$\begin{array}{r} 3\frac{33}{24} \\ -\ 2\frac{16}{24} \\ \hline 1\frac{17}{24} \end{array}$$

Directions   Subtract. Write your answer in simplest form.

1. $2\frac{1}{3} - 1\frac{5}{8}$ _____

2. $6\frac{3}{4} - 2\frac{1}{2}$ _____

3. $4\frac{3}{10} - 3\frac{13}{15}$ _____

4. $6\frac{7}{10} - 4\frac{9}{10}$ _____

5. $16\frac{1}{8} - 8\frac{3}{8}$ _____

6. $9\frac{3}{7} - 4\frac{6}{7}$ _____

7. $21\frac{9}{15} - 6\frac{14}{15}$ _____

8. $15\frac{3}{10} - 8\frac{1}{2}$ _____

9. $8\frac{3}{8} - 5\frac{3}{4}$ _____

10. $4\frac{1}{3} - 1\frac{5}{6}$ _____

11. $12\frac{15}{16} - 4\frac{3}{4}$ _____

12. $32\frac{4}{9} - 17\frac{13}{18}$ _____

Directions   Add or subtract.

13. Kerim jogged $3\frac{3}{4}$ miles on Thursday. On Friday, he jogged $\frac{2}{3}$ of a mile farther. How far did he jog on Friday? _____

14. Lejla caught a bass that was $1\frac{7}{8}$ pounds and a trout that was $3\frac{5}{8}$ pounds. How much heavier was the trout? _____

15. Mike studied $3\frac{1}{3}$ hours after school on Tuesday. On Wednesday, he studied $1\frac{3}{4}$ hours. How much longer did he study on Tuesday? _____

Multiplying Fractions and Mixed Numbers

EXAMPLE   Multiply $1\frac{2}{3} \cdot 2\frac{1}{2}$.

Step 1   Change the mixed numbers to improper fractions.

$1\frac{2}{3} = \frac{5}{3}$ $2\frac{1}{2} = \frac{5}{2}$

Step 2   Multiply the numerators and denominators.

$\frac{5}{3} \cdot \frac{5}{2} = \frac{5 \cdot 5}{3 \cdot 2} = \frac{25}{6}$

Step 3   Simplify. $\frac{25}{6} = 4\frac{1}{6}$

Directions   Multiply. Write your answer in simplest form.

1. $\frac{1}{5} \cdot \frac{5}{6}$ _____

2. $\frac{3}{4} \cdot \frac{4}{5}$ _____

3. $\frac{3}{8} \cdot \frac{2}{3}$ _____

4. $\frac{5}{9} \cdot \frac{9}{10}$ _____

5. $\frac{6}{7} \cdot \frac{1}{2}$ _____

6. $\frac{3}{7} \cdot \frac{7}{12}$ _____

7. $\frac{2}{9} \cdot \frac{3}{4}$ _____

8. $\frac{19}{20}y \cdot \frac{5}{6}x$ _____

9. $\frac{4}{5} \cdot \frac{5}{8}y$ _____

Directions   Multiply. Write your answer in simplest form.

10. $2\frac{3}{8} \cdot 1\frac{5}{19}$ _____

11. $1\frac{3}{4} \cdot 1\frac{6}{7}$ _____

12. $3\frac{1}{5} \cdot 1\frac{3}{16}$ _____

13. $4\frac{1}{2} \cdot 2\frac{1}{9}$ _____

14. $5\frac{1}{3} \cdot 2\frac{2}{5}$ _____

15. $3\frac{3}{4} \cdot 1\frac{3}{10}$ _____

16. $2\frac{5}{6} \cdot 3\frac{4}{17}a$ _____

17. $4\frac{4}{5}y \cdot 2\frac{7}{12}$ _____

18. $1\frac{2}{3}x \cdot 2\frac{7}{8}$ _____

Directions   Multiply to solve each problem. Write your answer in simplest form.

19. Four-fifths of Mrs. Martinez's class likes the color purple, while $\frac{7}{8}$ of Mr. Burns's class likes the color. What fraction of both classes like purple?

_____

20. Bobbie made a cake, which needed $4\frac{1}{3}$ cups of flour. Each cup weighs $8\frac{3}{4}$ ounces. How many ounces of flour did she use?

_____

Dividing Fractions and Mixed Numbers

EXAMPLE

Divide $1\frac{1}{3} \div 2\frac{1}{3}$.

Step 1 Change each mixed number into an improper fraction.

$$1\frac{1}{3} = \frac{4}{3} \qquad 2\frac{1}{3} = \frac{7}{3}$$

Step 2 Multiply the dividend by the reciprocal of the divisor.

$$\frac{4}{3} \div \frac{7}{3} \text{ becomes } \frac{4}{3} \cdot \frac{3}{7}.$$

$$\frac{4}{3} \cdot \frac{3}{7} = \frac{12}{21}$$

Step 3 If possible, simplify. $\frac{12}{21} = \frac{4}{7}$

Directions Divide. Write your answer in simplest form.

1. $\frac{5}{8} \div \frac{5}{6}$ _____

2. $\frac{1}{5} \div \frac{3}{4}$ _____

3. $\frac{7}{10} \div \frac{14}{15}$ _____

4. $\frac{3}{8} \div \frac{3}{5}$ _____

5. $\frac{7}{8} \div \frac{1}{2}$ _____

6. $\frac{9}{10} \div \frac{3}{8}$ _____

7. $\frac{1}{3} \div \frac{3}{7}$ _____

8. $\frac{6}{11n} \div \frac{4}{11}$ _____

9. $\frac{15}{16} \div \frac{5}{8y}$ _____

Directions Divide. Write your answer in simplest form.

10. $2\frac{2}{5} \div 1\frac{3}{5}$ _____

11. $6\frac{5}{8} \div 2\frac{1}{2}$ _____

12. $1\frac{2}{3} \div 1\frac{1}{4}$ _____

13. $3\frac{1}{3} \div 1\frac{1}{3}$ _____

14. $1\frac{3}{4} \div 2\frac{1}{2}$ _____

15. $4\frac{3}{8} \div 3\frac{1}{2}$ _____

16. $2\frac{2}{3} \div 5\frac{1}{3}$ _____

17. $1\frac{2}{7} \div 3\frac{6}{7}j$ _____

18. $5\frac{3}{8}w \div 1\frac{19}{24}$ _____

Directions Solve each problem. If necessary, reduce to simplest form.

19. Kelvin has a log that is $15\frac{1}{3}$ feet long. He must cut it into pieces that each measure $\frac{1}{2}$ foot. How many pieces can he cut?

_____

20. Melissa walked $12\frac{2}{3}$ miles in $2\frac{2}{3}$ hours. How many miles per hour did she walk?

_____

Using Fractions

Directions Complete the chart.

1. Sara surveyed 30 of her classmates for a
civics project. In the group, $\frac{1}{2}$ said they
watched TV for 2 hours every day. $\frac{1}{3}$ said
they watched for 1 hour. $\frac{1}{15}$ said they
watched for less than $\frac{1}{2}$ hour each day. The
rest of the group said they did not watch
television on a daily basis.

30 Classmates	How Many?
$\frac{1}{2}$ watch television 2 hours	_____
$\frac{1}{3}$ watch television 1 hour	_____
$\frac{1}{15}$ watch television $<\frac{1}{2}$ hour	_____
_____ do not watch daily	_____

Directions Solve each problem.

2. Mike can walk a mile in $\frac{2}{3}$ of an hour. Dennis can walk a mile in $\frac{5}{8}$ of an
hour. Who walks a mile faster? _____

3. On Wednesday, Elaine told Sam she finished $\frac{7}{8}$ of her science project.
Sam said he finished $\frac{15}{16}$. Who has finished more of the project? _____

4. Kendra lives $\frac{6}{7}$ of a mile from the mall. Ali lives $\frac{5}{9}$ of a mile from the mall.
Who lives closer to the mall? _____

5. To go to the video store, Jennifer walks $2\frac{5}{8}$ blocks north and $4\frac{1}{2}$
blocks east. How many blocks does she walk to the video store? _____

6. To build a birdhouse, Pat needs $16\frac{5}{8}$ inches of pine and $9\frac{2}{3}$ inches
of cedar. How many more inches of pine does she need? _____

7. Darlene walked for $2\frac{3}{8}$ hours at $3\frac{2}{3}$ miles per hour. How many miles
did she walk? _____

8. Grass seed costs $3.50 ($3\frac{1}{2}$) a pound. Frank needs $2\frac{1}{2}$ pounds of
grass seed. How much will the grass seed cost? _____

9. Jack and Bill disagreed over their homework. Jack said
$10\frac{1}{3} \cdot 4\frac{7}{8} = 50\frac{3}{8}$. Is he correct? _____

10. At lunch, Ti's restaurant sells 150 sandwiches. $\frac{3}{5}$ of the sandwiches are beef,
$\frac{3}{10}$ are chicken, and $\frac{1}{25}$ are cheese. The rest of the sandwiches are ham.
How many ham sandwiches are sold? _____

The Order of Operations

EXAMPLE

$5(3 + 2) - 8 \div 4$

Step 1 Do the operation inside the parentheses.

$5(5) - 8 \div 4$

Step 2 Multiply and divide from left to right.

$25 - 2$

Step 3 Subtract.

$25 - 2 = 23$

Directions Simplify each expression using the order of operations.

1. $16 - 5 \cdot 3$ _____

2. $9 + 11 \cdot 2$ _____

3. $4(6 - 3)$ _____

4. $8(42 \div 7)$ _____

5. $3 + 5(20 - 18)$ _____

6. $(4 \cdot 2) \div 2 + 10$ _____

7. $25 - 4(10 - 4)$ _____

8. $3 + 4 \cdot 5 - 12 \div 4$ _____

9. $7 \cdot 6 + 20 \div 10$ _____

10. $20 - 10 \div 2 \cdot 3$ _____

11. $9(1 + 4) - 3 \cdot 8$ _____

12. $35 \div (5 \cdot 7) + 1$ _____

13. $25(8 \div 2) - 10(22 - 19)$ _____

14. $15 \div 3 \div 5 + 6$ _____

15. $8 + 28 \div 7$ _____

16. $9 - 12 \div 4 + 2$ _____

17. $6 \cdot 2 + 25 \div 5$ _____

18. $8(6 - 3) - 4 \div 2$ _____

19. $16 \div (2 \cdot 2) - 3$ _____

20. $20(20 \div 4) + 3 - 2$ _____

Directions Use a calculator to simplify each expression.

21. $100 - 8 \cdot 7 + 23$ _____

22. $7(625 \div 25) - 4 \cdot 5 \cdot 5$ _____

23. $32 \div 4(62 - 60)$ _____

24. $16 + 5 \cdot 7 - 81 \div 9 + 30$ _____

25. $20 + 12(169 \div 13) \div 6$ _____

26. $42 \div 7 + 6(154 \div 11)$ _____

27. $97 - 128 \div 4 \cdot 3$ _____

28. $(18 + 6) \div 4 \cdot 10$ _____

29. $19 - 3 \cdot 2 \cdot 8 \div 6$ _____

30. $45 + 10(32 - 32) + 40$ _____

Evaluating Algebraic Expressions

EXAMPLE

Evaluate $5y + 2$, when $y = 1, 2, 3$.

When $y = 1$:

$5(1) + 2 =$

$5 + 2 = 7$

When $y = 2$:

$5(2) + 2 =$

$10 + 2 = 12$

When $y = 3$:

$5(3) + 2 =$

$15 + 2 = 17$

Directions Evaluate each expression for $n = 6$.

1. $n + 4$ _____

2. $n - 3$ _____

3. $42 - 3n$ _____

4. $5n + 2$ _____

5. $14 + \frac{n}{3}$ _____

6. $\frac{n}{2} - 1$ _____

7. $4n - 13$ _____

8. $2 + \frac{n}{4}$ _____

9. $\frac{5}{2n} + \frac{3}{3n}$ _____

10. $3n - 2n$ _____

Directions Evaluate each expression for $y = 7$.

11. $y + 3$ _____

12. $2y - 10$ _____

13. $21 - 3y$ _____

14. $6y + 1$ _____

15. $12 + \frac{y}{7}$ _____

16. $\frac{y}{3} - 1$ _____

17. $4y - 16$ _____

18. $6 + \frac{1}{y}$ _____

19. $\frac{2}{3y} + \frac{2y}{3}$ _____

20. $4y + 2y$ _____

Directions Evaluate each expression for $z = 10$.

21. $4z - 12$ _____

22. $z + 8$ _____

23. $52 - 5z$ _____

24. $3z + 4$ _____

25. $11 + \frac{z}{2}$ _____

26. $\frac{z}{3} - 1$ _____

27. $5z - 3z$ _____

28. $1 + \frac{1}{z}$ _____

29. $3\frac{z}{5} + \frac{5}{z}$ _____

30. $z + 2z$ _____

Equations—Solution by Substitution

Substitute numbers into $2x + 3 = 13$ to find the root of the equation.

Substitute 0 for the variable.

$2(0) + 3 = 13$

$3 = 13$ is false.

When $x = 5$, $2x + 3 = 13$ is true.

Therefore, $x = 5$ is true.

Directions   Substitute numbers into each equation to find the root of the equation.

1. $6x + 1 = 19$ _____

2. $12x - 4 = 44$ _____

3. $28 - 2x = 14$ _____

4. $\frac{1}{2}x + 2 = 7$ _____

5. $3 + 4x = 3$ _____

6. $9 \cdot x = 27$ _____

7. $6 + 4x = 26$ _____

8. $15 - 6x = 3$ _____

9. $7x - 14 = 14$ _____

10. $x \cdot 5 = 35$ _____

11. $2 + 3x = 8$ _____

12. $x + x = 10$ _____

13. $4x - 4 = 20$ _____

14. $60 - 2x = 40$ _____

15. $\frac{5}{8}x + \frac{3}{8} = 1$ _____

16. $2x + 13 = 25$ _____

17. $10 - 3x = 1$ _____

18. $23 - 4x = 15$ _____

19. $20x - 15 = 65$ _____

20. $\frac{1}{2}x + 3 = 7$ _____

21. $5 + 3x = 26$ _____

22. $8 \cdot x = 72$ _____

23. $2 + 6x = 62$ _____

24. $x \cdot 4 = 8$ _____

25. $x - 3 = 1$ _____

Solving Addition Equations

EXAMPLE

Solve $5 + x = 16$ for x.

Step 1 Subtract 5 from each side.

$5 + x - 5 = 16 - 5$

Step 2 Perform the operations.

$x = 11$

Step 3 Check by substitution.

$5 + 11 = 16$ is true.

Directions Solve for each variable. Write your answer in simplest form. Check each solution.

1. $a + 11 = 17$ _____

2. $x + 16 = 38$ _____

3. $42 + y = 72$ _____

4. $29 + b = 46$ _____

5. $x + 19 = 37$ _____

6. $n + 16 = 32$ _____

7. $x + 9 = 29$ _____

8. $19 + m = 30$ _____

9. $67 + x = 72$ _____

10. $v + 15 = 28$ _____

11. $c + 7 = 28$ _____

12. $36 + e = 59$ _____

13. $w + \frac{5}{8} = 1$ _____

14. $\frac{1}{2} + b = \frac{11}{16}$ _____

15. $\frac{1}{3} + f = \frac{5}{6}$ _____

16. $x + \frac{3}{4} = \frac{7}{8}$ _____

17. $\frac{4}{5} + t = 1\frac{2}{5}$ _____

18. $c + \frac{1}{5} = \frac{13}{15}$ _____

19. $j + \frac{1}{5} = 1$ _____

20. $\frac{1}{2} = \frac{1}{3} + g$ _____

21. $\frac{7}{8} = \frac{5}{8} + p$ _____

22. $1\frac{3}{8} = y + \frac{5}{8}$ _____

23. $1\frac{2}{15} = \frac{4}{5} + d$ _____

24. $\frac{1}{2} = s + \frac{1}{4}$ _____

25. $\frac{5}{6} = h + \frac{1}{6}$ _____

Solving Subtraction Equations

EXAMPLE

Solve $x - \frac{1}{2} = \frac{3}{4}$ for x.

Step 1 Isolate the variable x by adding the inverse.

$$x - \frac{1}{2} + \frac{1}{2} = \frac{3}{4} + \frac{1}{2}$$

Step 2 Perform each operation.

$$x - \frac{1}{2} + \frac{1}{2} = \frac{3}{4} + \frac{2}{4}$$

$$x = \frac{5}{4}$$

Step 3 Simplify if necessary.

$$x = 1\frac{1}{4}$$

Directions Solve for each variable. Write your answer in simplest form.

1. $x - 13 = 25$ _____

2. $y - 7 = 8$ _____

3. $a - 19 = 23$ _____

4. $d - 9 = 2$ _____

5. $e - 17 = 33$ _____

6. $s - 25 = 42$ _____

7. $t - 18 = 20$ _____

8. $n - 23 = 49$ _____

9. $f - 16 = 39$ _____

10. $g - \frac{1}{4} = \frac{1}{4}$ _____

11. $v - \frac{3}{8} = \frac{1}{4}$ _____

12. $c - \frac{1}{6} = \frac{1}{2}$ _____

13. $z - \frac{3}{16} = \frac{9}{16}$ _____

14. $n - \frac{1}{2} = \frac{3}{8}$ _____

15. $h - \frac{5}{8} = \frac{5}{8}$ _____

16. $x - \frac{1}{2} = \frac{7}{16}$ _____

17. $j - \frac{3}{10} = \frac{3}{5}$ _____

18. $x - \frac{1}{10} = \frac{3}{10}$ _____

Directions Use addition or subtraction to solve these problems.

19. The United States and Canada produced 16 million ounces of gold. Canada alone produced 5 million ounces of gold. How much gold did the U.S. produce?

20. Mexico and Congo produced 578 thousand ounces of gold. Congo produced 257 thousand ounces of gold. How much gold did Mexico produce?

_____ _____

Complex Fractions

EXAMPLE

Simplify $\dfrac{\frac{2}{3}}{\frac{2}{5}}$.

Step 1 Rewrite the complex fraction horizontally $\dfrac{\frac{2}{3}}{\frac{2}{5}} = \frac{2}{3} \div \frac{2}{5}$

Step 2 To divide, multiply the dividend by the reciprocal of the divisor.

$$\frac{2}{3} \div \frac{2}{5} = \frac{2}{3} \bullet \frac{5}{2} = \frac{10}{6} \qquad \text{or} \qquad \dfrac{\frac{2}{3} \bullet \left(\frac{5}{2}\right)}{\frac{2}{5} \bullet \left(\frac{5}{2}\right)} = \dfrac{\frac{2}{3} \bullet \frac{5}{2}}{1} = \frac{2}{3} \bullet \frac{5}{2} = \frac{10}{6}$$

Step 3 Simplify.

$$\frac{10}{6} = 1\frac{4}{6} = 1\frac{2}{3}$$

Directions   Simplify each complex fraction.

1. $\dfrac{\frac{2}{3}}{\frac{1}{3}}$ _____

2. $\dfrac{\frac{5}{8}}{\frac{3}{4}}$ _____

3. $\dfrac{\frac{1}{5}}{\frac{3}{8}}$ _____

4. $\dfrac{\frac{15}{16}}{\frac{1}{8}}$ _____

5. $\dfrac{6}{\frac{2}{3}}$ _____

6. $\dfrac{\frac{4}{5}}{\frac{4}{9}}$ _____

7. $\dfrac{\frac{6}{7}}{\frac{5}{7}}$ _____

8. $\dfrac{\frac{3}{8}}{\frac{3}{4}}$ _____

9. $\dfrac{\frac{7}{9}}{\frac{7}{8}}$ _____

10. $\dfrac{\frac{3}{4}}{6}$ _____

11. $\dfrac{7}{\frac{3}{8}}$ _____

12. $\dfrac{\frac{5}{9}}{\frac{2}{3}}$ _____

13. $\dfrac{1}{\frac{3}{10}}$ _____

14. $\dfrac{\frac{3}{5}}{\frac{9}{10}}$ _____

15. $\dfrac{\frac{1}{2}}{\frac{7}{8}}$ _____

16. $\dfrac{\frac{5}{6}}{\frac{2}{3}}$ _____

17. $\dfrac{8}{\frac{4}{11}}$ _____

18. $\dfrac{\frac{2}{5}}{\frac{7}{10}}$ _____

19. $\dfrac{4}{\frac{2}{3}}$ _____

20. $\dfrac{\frac{7}{9}}{3}$ _____

21. $\dfrac{\frac{1}{4}}{\frac{3}{4}}$ _____

22. $\dfrac{16}{\frac{5}{8}}$ _____

23. $\dfrac{\frac{4}{5}}{\frac{5}{14}}$ _____

24. $\dfrac{\frac{1}{2}}{6}$ _____

25. $\dfrac{5}{\frac{1}{3}}$ _____

Simplifying by Addition

EXAMPLE

Simplify $\frac{3x}{8} + \frac{5x}{12}$.

Step 1 Find the LCM of the denominators.

LCM = 24

Step 2 Write equivalent fractions.

$$\frac{3x \cdot 3}{8 \cdot 3} + \frac{5x \cdot 2}{12 \cdot 2} = \frac{9x}{24} + \frac{10x}{24}$$

Step 3 Add the equivalent fractions.

$$\frac{9x}{24} + \frac{10x}{24} = \frac{19x}{24}$$

Step 4 Simplify if possible. $\frac{19x}{24}$ is in simplest form.

Directions Simplify. Write your answer in simplest form.

1. $\frac{1}{5x} + \frac{2}{5x}$ _____

2. $\frac{2c}{4} + \frac{1c}{4}$ _____

3. $\frac{5}{8y} + \frac{2}{8y}$ _____

4. $\frac{4b}{7} + \frac{6b}{7}$ _____

5. $\frac{3z}{5} + \frac{4z}{5}$ _____

6. $\frac{3}{8j} + \frac{2}{8j}$ _____

7. $\frac{3w}{10} + \frac{2w}{10}$ _____

8. $\frac{3}{4x} + \frac{3}{4x}$ _____

9. $\frac{13d}{16} + \frac{3d}{16}$ _____

10. $\frac{5}{9y} + \frac{2}{9y}$ _____

11. $\frac{4g}{5} + \frac{1g}{5}$ _____

12. $\frac{1}{4b} + \frac{1}{4b}$ _____

13. $\frac{3}{10q} + \frac{9}{10q}$ _____

14. $\frac{5x}{8} + \frac{7x}{8}$ _____

15. $\frac{2}{11p} + \frac{5}{11p}$ _____

Directions Simplify by collecting like terms. Write your answer in simplest form.

16. $\frac{2}{5c} + \frac{1}{3c}$ _____

17. $\frac{5b}{8} + \frac{3b}{16}$ _____

18. $\frac{1y}{4} + \frac{2y}{3}$ _____

19. $\frac{2}{3j} + \frac{11}{12j}$ _____

20. $\frac{3}{5r} + \frac{1}{6r}$ _____

21. $\frac{2e}{7} + \frac{5e}{14}$ _____

22. $\frac{5}{12k} + \frac{3}{4k}$ _____

23. $\frac{7}{9m} + \frac{2}{3m}$ _____

24. $\frac{2n}{9} + \frac{1n}{3}$ _____

25. $\frac{1}{5v} + \frac{3}{4v}$ _____

Simplifying by Subtraction

EXAMPLE Simplify $\frac{b}{2} - \frac{b}{5}$.

Step 1 Find the LCM of the denominators.   LCM = 10

Step 2 Write equivalent fractions. $\frac{b \cdot 5}{2 \cdot 5} - \frac{b \cdot 2}{5 \cdot 2} = \frac{5b}{10} - \frac{2b}{10}$

Step 3 Subtract the equivalent fractions. $\frac{5b}{10} - \frac{2b}{10} = \frac{3b}{10}$

Step 4 Simplify if possible. $\frac{3b}{10}$ is in simplest form.

Directions Simplify. Write your answer in simplest form.

1. $\frac{5c}{8} - \frac{3c}{8}$ _____

2. $\frac{3}{4d} - \frac{1}{4d}$ _____

3. $\frac{3w}{5} - \frac{2w}{5}$ _____

4. $\frac{15}{16e} - \frac{7}{16e}$ _____

5. $\frac{11}{14h} - \frac{5}{14h}$ _____

6. $\frac{9g}{10} - \frac{3g}{10}$ _____

7. $\frac{5}{6s} - \frac{1}{6s}$ _____

8. $\frac{7b}{9} - \frac{4b}{9}$ _____

9. $\frac{2}{3q} - \frac{1}{3q}$ _____

Directions Simplify by collecting like terms. Write your answer in simplest form.

10. $\frac{9}{10a} - \frac{1}{2a}$ _____

11. $\frac{8c}{9} - \frac{2c}{3}$ _____

12. $\frac{5p}{16} - \frac{1p}{4}$ _____

13. $\frac{2}{3r} - \frac{5}{8r}$ _____

14. $\frac{4x}{5} - \frac{5x}{8}$ _____

15. $\frac{3s}{4} - \frac{7s}{16}$ _____

16. $\frac{5}{9k} - \frac{1}{3k}$ _____

17. $\frac{11y}{16} - \frac{1y}{2}$ _____

Directions Solve these problems.

18. Ed spends $\frac{3}{8}$ of his study time on history. How much of his study time does he have left?

_____

19. Juan has $\frac{7}{8}$ yards of string. He used $\frac{2}{3}$ yards of string. How much does he have left?

_____

20. Jenny's survey showed that $\frac{11}{16}$ of her class picked blue as their favorite color. What part of her class picked a different color?

_____

Multiplying Rational Expressions

EXAMPLE

Multiply $\frac{5}{8} \cdot \frac{2}{5}$.

Step 1 Multiply the numerators and the denominators.

$$\frac{5}{8} \cdot \frac{2}{5} = \frac{5 \cdot 2}{8 \cdot 5} = \frac{10}{40}$$

Step 2 If possible, simplify the fraction.

$$\frac{10}{40} = \frac{1}{4}$$

Directions Multiply. Write your answer in simplest form.

1. $\frac{3}{4} \cdot \frac{4}{5}$ _____

2. $\frac{5}{8} \cdot \frac{8}{9}$ _____

3. $\frac{14}{15} \cdot \frac{5}{7}$ _____

4. $\frac{9}{10} \cdot \frac{5}{6}$ _____

5. $\frac{6}{7} \cdot \frac{14}{15}$ _____

6. $\frac{1}{5} \cdot \frac{8}{9}$ _____

7. $\frac{2}{3} \cdot \frac{3}{4}$ _____

8. $\frac{8}{11} \cdot \frac{11}{12}$ _____

9. $\frac{5}{12} \cdot \frac{24}{25}$ _____

10. $\frac{1}{9} \cdot \frac{2}{3}$ _____

11. $\frac{5}{16} \cdot \frac{8}{9}$ _____

12. $\frac{1}{2s} \cdot \frac{1}{6}$ _____

13. $\frac{4v}{7} \cdot \frac{7}{16v}$ _____

14. $\frac{7}{8} \cdot \frac{16g}{17}$ _____

15. $\frac{3}{8c} \cdot \frac{7c}{21}$ _____

16. $\frac{4}{5} \cdot \frac{10}{11d}$ _____

17. $\frac{7}{15m} \cdot \frac{5}{7}$ _____

18. $\frac{9}{10n} \cdot \frac{2n}{3}$ _____

19. $\frac{9x}{13} \cdot \frac{13}{27}$ _____

20. $\frac{5}{6a} \cdot \frac{1a}{2}$ _____

21. $\frac{4b}{15} \cdot \frac{5}{6}$ _____

22. $\frac{8v}{9} \cdot \frac{1}{2v}$ _____

Directions Solve each problem. Write your answer in simplest form.

23. Glenn has $\frac{2}{5}$ of a granola bar. If he eats $\frac{7}{8}$ of it, how much of the granola bar is left?

_____

24. Amanda pours $\frac{2}{9}$ of a bag of pretzels into a dish. She eats $\frac{1}{2}$ of the pretzels in the dish. How much of the bag did she eat?

_____

25. The Jordan River is $\frac{1}{3}$ the length of the Tisza River. The Tisza River is 600 miles long. How long is the Jordan River?

_____

Ratios

EXAMPLE

A ratio is a comparison of two quantities using fractions.

Here are some ways to write a ratio: $\frac{3}{8}$ 3 to 8   3:8

Express a ratio in simplest form.

$\frac{10}{24} = \frac{10 \div 2}{24 \div 2} = \frac{5}{12}$ 5 to 12   or   5:12

Directions Complete the chart to show how to write each ratio two other ways.

1. $\frac{8}{13}$		
2.	4 to 11	
3.		5:17
4.	16 to 9	
5. $\frac{12}{7}$		
6.		21:14
7. $\frac{11}{15}$		
8.	27 to 41	
9.		37:19
10.	53 to 61	

Directions Write *OK* if each ratio is a fraction expressed in its simplest form. If the fraction is *not* expressed in its simplest form, write the simplest form.

11. $\frac{5}{15}$ _____   **16.** $\frac{14}{56}$ _____

12. $\frac{2}{5}$ _____   **17.** $\frac{32}{57}$ _____

13. $\frac{6}{8}$ _____   **18.** $\frac{9}{24}$ _____

14. $\frac{3}{24}$ _____   **19.** $\frac{7}{15}$ _____

15. $\frac{17}{25}$ _____   **20.** $\frac{32}{9}$ _____

Proportions

A proportion is an equation made up of two equal ratios: $\frac{a}{b} = \frac{c}{d}$

A proportion is a true proportion if this equation is true: $ad = bc$.

The terms ad and bc are called cross products and can be used to solve for a missing variable.

$\frac{16}{24} = \frac{2}{n}$ $(16)(n) = (24)(2)$ $16(n) = 48$ $n = 3$

Directions Write *yes* or *no* to show whether each proportion is a true proportion.

1. $\frac{6}{13} = \frac{18}{39}$ _____

3. $\frac{9}{12} = \frac{3}{5}$ _____

5. $\frac{10}{16} = \frac{5}{8}$ _____

2. $\frac{2}{7} = \frac{4}{13}$ _____

4. $\frac{4}{16} = \frac{1}{4}$ _____

6. $\frac{5}{8} = \frac{40}{64}$ _____

Directions Write the proportions as an equation of cross products.

7. $\frac{2}{3} = \frac{6}{x}$ _____

10. $\frac{x}{12} = \frac{30}{72}$ _____

8. $\frac{1}{9} = \frac{b}{81}$ _____

11. $\frac{42}{48} = \frac{t}{8}$ _____

9. $\frac{6}{c} = \frac{36}{42}$ _____

12. $\frac{3}{8} = \frac{30}{w}$ _____

Directions Solve for the variable in each proportion.

13. $\frac{2}{5} = \frac{x}{20}$ _____

17. $\frac{4}{15} = \frac{d}{75}$ _____

14. $\frac{3}{8} = \frac{c}{24}$ _____

18. $\frac{3}{4} = \frac{6}{y}$ _____

15. $\frac{5}{w} = \frac{1}{5}$ _____

19. $\frac{3}{1} = \frac{x}{4}$ _____

16. $\frac{6}{9} = \frac{12}{a}$ _____

20. $\frac{c}{3} = \frac{28}{21}$ _____

Ratios and Proportions

EXAMPLE A table can be helpful in solving proportion problems.

A record store sold 1 tape for every 5 CDs. If 60 CDs were sold, how many tapes were sold?

Number of Tapes	1	x
Number of CDs	5	60

Write an equation and solve it.

$\frac{1}{5} = \frac{x}{60}$ $(1)(60) = (5)(x)$ $60 = 5x$ $x = 12$

Directions Fill in each chart. Solve the problem.

1. Three cans of peas cost $1.80. How much do 9 cans cost? _____

Number of Cans		
Cost		

2. A soccer player averaged 1 goal for every 18 tries. If the player made 6 goals, how many tries were made? _____

Goals		
Tries		

3. A bag of pecans has 2 broken pecans for each 84 nuts. How many broken pecans were found in a sack of 504 nuts? _____

Number of Broken Pecans		
Total Nuts		

4. In a class, two out of every nine students were left-handed. How many left-handers would be found in a group of 63 students? _____

Left-handers		
Total Students		

5. If 20 pounds of bird seed cost $4.40, how much would 3 pounds cost? _____

Number of Pounds		
Cost		

Proportional Relationships

EXAMPLE A bag of crackers has $2\frac{1}{2}$ servings. One serving size of crackers contains 7 grams of fat. How many grams of fat are in the whole bag of crackers?

     STEP 1   Set up a proportion.

$$\frac{\text{Bag}}{\text{number of servings}} = \frac{1}{2\frac{1}{2}}$$

     STEP 2   Name the unknown.

                  x = total grams of fat

     STEP 3   Cross multiply. Solve for x.

$$\frac{7}{x} = \frac{1}{2\frac{1}{2}}$$

                  $x = 17\frac{1}{2}$ total grams of fat

There are $17\frac{1}{2}$ grams of fat in one bag of crackers.

Directions Solve each problem using a proportion.

1. Sarah hopes to be as tall as her older sister. Her sister is 70 inches tall. Sarah is only half as tall. How tall is Sarah?

   _____

2. Raphael is going to meet Pete at the park to play baseball. Raphael walks 65 feet to the park. Pete walks 3 times as far as Raphael walked. How far does Pete walk?

   _____

3. Marisa's father can lift 180 pounds. Marisa's brother can lift $\frac{1}{3}$ of what their father can lift. How much weight can Marisa's brother lift?

   _____

4. One tow truck can pull 2,500 pounds. Another tow truck can pull 7,500 pounds. What is the weight limit ratio between the two trucks?

   _____

5. June bought a container of juice that held 2 quarts. Juanita bought a container that held 2 times more juice. How much juice did Juanita buy?

   _____

Solving Distance, Rate, and Time Problems

EXAMPLE

The distance formula is $d = rt$.

d stands for **distance**, r for **rate** of speed, and t for **time**.

Find d when $r = 20$ kilometers per hour (km/h) and $t = 2$ hours.

Solve: $d = (20)(2) = 40$ kilometers

Use $r = \frac{d}{t}$ to solve for rate of speed.

Find r when $d = 33$ miles and $t = 3$ hours.

Solve: $r = \frac{33}{3} = 11$ miles per hour (mph)

Use $t = \frac{d}{r}$ to solve for total time.

Find t when $d = 450$ kilometers and $r = 90$ km/h.

Solve: $t = \frac{450}{90} = 5$ hours

Directions Use the appropriate version of the distance formula to find the unknown value.

1. $d = ?$ $r = 5$ mph $t = \frac{1}{2}$ hour   Answer in miles. _____

2. $d = ?$ $r = 38$ km/h $t = 3$ hours   Answer in kilometers. _____

3. $d = 90$ miles $r = 60$ mph $t = ?$ Answer in hours. _____

4. $d = 1{,}968$ kilometers $r = ?$ $t = 24$ hours   Answer in km/h. _____

5. $d = 54$ miles $r = 18$ mph $t = ?$ Answer in hours. _____

6. $d = ?$ $r = 27$ km/h $t = \frac{1}{3}$ hour   Answer in kilometers. _____

7. $d = 332$ kilometers $r = ?$ $t = 4$ hours   Answer in km/h. _____

8. $d = 14$ miles $r = 70$ mph $t = ?$ Answer in hours. _____

9. $d = 1{,}233$ miles $r = ?$ $t = 3$ hours   Answer in mph. _____

10. $d = ?$ $r = 96$ km/h $t = \frac{3}{4}$ hour   Answer in kilometers. _____

Percents and Fractions

EXAMPLE	A percent is a ratio based on the number 100.

29 percent means 29 parts of a 100.

It can be written $\frac{29}{100}$ or 29%.

Directions Write a fraction to show the percent of each shaded square.

1.

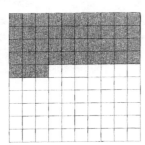

_____

2.

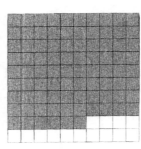

_____

3.

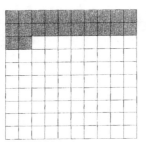

_____

4.

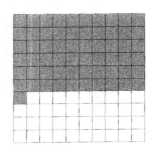

_____

Directions Shade in the following percents.

5. 8%

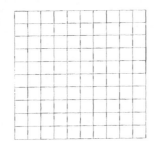

6. 25%

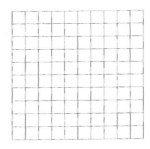

7. 87%

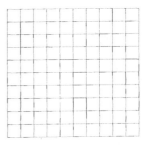

8. 43%

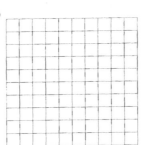

9. 92%

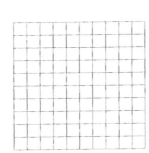

10. 12%

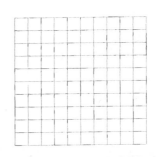

Percents and Decimals

EXAMPLE

Change a decimal to a percent.   0.35 to 35%   0.07 to 7%

Change a percent to a decimal.   46% to $\frac{46}{100}$ to 0.46

Change a fraction to a percent. $\frac{46}{100}$ to 46%

Change a fraction with a denominator that is not 100.

$\frac{3}{4}$ to 3 ÷ 4 to 0.75 to 75%

Directions Complete the chart by filling in the missing numbers.

	Decimal	Percent	Fraction
1.		63%	
2.			$\frac{2}{5}$
3.	0.10		
4.		25%	
5.			$\frac{51}{100}$
6.	0.41		
7.		55%	
8.	0.67		
9.			$\frac{9}{25}$
10.			$\frac{17}{20}$
11.	0.50		
12.		93%	
13.			$\frac{21}{50}$
14.			$\frac{7}{20}$
15.		88%	

More Percents and Decimals

Directions Change each fraction to a percent.

1. $\frac{1}{10}$ _____

2. $\frac{4}{5}$ _____

3. $\frac{1}{2}$ _____

4. $\frac{7}{8}$ _____

5. $\frac{1}{5}$ _____

6. $\frac{3}{5}$ _____

7. $\frac{1}{4}$ _____

8. $\frac{17}{25}$ _____

9. $\frac{3}{8}$ _____

10. $\frac{7}{16}$ _____

Directions Change each percent above to a decimal.

11. _____

12. _____

13. _____

14. _____

15. _____

16. _____

17. _____

18. _____

19. _____

20. _____

Directions Read each problem and write a percent *and* a decimal for the fraction used in the problem. Then solve the problem.

21. One-third of a school's students went to the football game. There are 270 students in the school. How many students attended the game? _____

22. Two-fifths of a school's 640 students eat a school lunch each day. How many students eat school lunches each day? _____

23. Of the 200 trees in the park, five-eighths are by the lake. How many trees are by the lake? _____

24. Three-tenths of the birds in the zoo live in the rainforest. The zoo has 470 birds. How many of the zoo's birds live in the rainforest? _____

25. Nine hundred people visit the elephants every day. That is three-fourths of the visitors to the zoo. How many people visit the zoo each day? _____

Finding the Percent of a Number

EXAMPLE

Here are some ways to find the percent of a number:

20% of 400

Use a proportion.　　$\frac{20}{100} = \frac{x}{400}$　to　(20)(400) = (100)(x)　to　8,000 = 100x　to　x = 80

Use the 1% solution.　100% = 400　to　$\frac{100\%}{100} = \frac{400}{100}$

1% of 400 is 4.

1% • 20 = 4 • 20　20% = 80

Use an equation.　　(20%)(400) = (.20)(400) = 80

Directions　Find the percent. Fill in the missing number to complete each equation. Then solve it.

1. 75% of 16　　(75%)(　　) = (　　)(16) = _____

2. 30% of 30　　(　　)(30) = (0.30)(　　) = _____

3. 26% of 55　　(26%)(　　) = (　　)(55) = _____

4. 93% of 70　　(　　)(70) = (0.93)(　　) = _____

5. 77% of 42　　(77%)(　　) = (　　)(42) = _____

Directions　Find the percent of each number.

6. 20% of 40　　_____

7. 25% of 120　　_____

8. 35% of 70　　_____

9. 60% of 80　　_____

10. 81% of 25　　_____

11. 12% of 53　　_____

12. 78% of 36　　_____

13. 90% of 56　　_____

14. 80% of 223　　_____

15. 45% of 390　　_____

Finding the Percent

EXAMPLE

What percent of 800 is 200?

Here are some ways to find out.

Use a ratio. $\frac{200}{800} = \frac{x}{100}$ to $(200)(100) = (800)(x)$ to $20,000 = 800x$ to $x = 25\%$

Use the 1% solution. $100\% = 800$ to $\frac{100\%}{100} = \frac{800}{100}$

$1\% = 8$ $\frac{200}{8} = 25\%$

Use an equation. $(x)(800) = 200$ to $800x = 200$ to $x = \frac{2}{8} = \frac{1}{4} = 25\%$

Directions Find the missing percent.

1. 15 is _____% of 20.

2. 64 is _____% of 320.

3. 48 is _____% of 96.

4. 300 is _____% of 120.

5. 44 is _____% of 11.

6. 900 is _____% of 45.

Directions Find the given percentage of each number.

	18% of	26% of	73% of
21	**7.** _____	**8.** _____	**9.** _____
73	**10.** _____	**11.** _____	**12.** _____
65	**13.** _____	**14.** _____	**15.** _____
56	**16.** _____	**17.** _____	**18.** _____
82	**19.** _____	**20.** _____	**21.** _____
37	**22.** _____	**23.** _____	**24.** _____
28	**25.** _____	**26.** _____	**27.** _____
45	**28.** _____	**29.** _____	**30.** _____

Percent of Increase and Decrease

EXAMPLE

A plant grew from 6 inches to 24 inches. By what percent did it increase?

To find an increase: Subtract. $24 - 6 = 18$

Write and solve an equation.   18 inches is what percent of 6 inches?

$\frac{\text{amount of increase}}{\text{original amount}} = \frac{18}{6} = x$ $x = 3 = 300\%$

There were 200 towels on a roll. Now there are 184 sheets.
What was the percent of decrease?

To find the decrease: Subtract. $200 - 184 = 16$

Write a proportion and solve.

$\frac{\text{amount of decrease}}{\text{total}} = \frac{x}{100}$ $\frac{16}{200} = \frac{x}{100}$ $(16)(100) = (200)(x)$ $1,600 = 200x$ $x = 8\%$

Directions Solve each increase or decrease problem.

From	Amount of Increase	Percent of Increase
1. 120 to 200	_____	_____
2. 85 to 105	_____	_____
3. 60 to 72	_____	_____
4. 123 to 265	_____	_____
5. 212 to 316	_____	_____
6. 87 to 93	_____	_____
7. 212 to 444	_____	_____

From	Amount of Decrease	Percent of Decrease
8. 210 to 156	_____	_____
9. 84 to 64	_____	_____
10. 168 to 46	_____	_____
11. 454 to 360	_____	_____
12. 15 to 3	_____	_____
13. 344 to 268	_____	_____
14. 92 to 76	_____	_____
15. 212 to 146	_____	_____

Formulas and Percents

EXAMPLE The formula for compound interest involves percents.

$A = P(1 + i)^n$

A = amount of money $A = \$200(1 + 0.04)^2$

P = principal or original deposit $A = \$200(1.04)^2$

i = interest rate per period (shown as a decimal) $A = \$200(1.0816)$

n = number of compounding periods $A = \$216.32$

Directions Write each percentage rate as a decimal.

1. $3\frac{3}{4}$ _____

4. $1\frac{1}{4}$ _____

7. $5\frac{1}{2}$ _____

2. $4\frac{1}{4}$ _____

5. $3\frac{1}{3}$ _____

8. $4\frac{1}{4}$ _____

3. $2\frac{1}{2}$ _____

6. $2\frac{3}{4}$ _____

9. $8\frac{3}{4}$ _____

Directions Solve each problem. Round to the fourth digit.

10. $(1.04)^3$ _____

13. $(1.0375)^2$ _____

11. $(1.034)^2$ _____

14. $(1.0875)^3$ _____

12. $(1.0425)^2$ _____

15. $(1.025)^2$ _____

Directions Solve each problem.

A bank advertised an interest rate on a savings account of $3\frac{1}{2}$% annually. How much did each person have at the end of two years?

Original Deposit	Amount After Two Years
16. $250	_____
17. $1,800	_____
18. $735	_____
19. $2,145	_____
20. $8,620	_____

Scale Drawings and Models

EXAMPLE   Find the missing value in the pair of similar shapes.

STEP 1   Set up a proportion.

$$\frac{x}{12} = \frac{4}{8}$$

STEP 2   Cross multiply. Solve for x.

$$8x = 48$$

$$x = 6$$

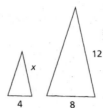

Directions   Find the missing value in each pair of similar shapes.

1. _____

2. _____

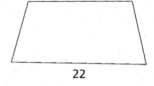

3. _____

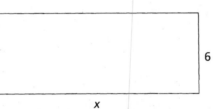

EXAMPLE   Helen wants to scale down a drawing she scanned onto her computer.
The current size of the drawing is 4 inches long by $5\frac{1}{2}$ inches wide.
Helen wants the new length to be 2 inches. What will the new width be?

STEP 1   Set up a proportion.   **STEP 3**   Cross multiply. Solve for x.

$$\frac{4}{5\frac{1}{2}} = \frac{\text{length}}{\text{width}} \qquad\qquad \frac{4}{5\frac{1}{2}} = \frac{2}{x}$$

STEP 2   Name the unknown. $x = 2\frac{3}{4}$

         x = new width   The new width will be $2\frac{3}{4}$ inches.

Directions   Solve each problem.

4. A building is 75 feet tall but is drawn
3 inches tall in a book. What is the scale of
the height of the drawing in the book to
the height of the real building?

5. Robin has a scale drawing of her living room.
The room is 12 feet long by 13 feet wide.
What will the size of the drawing of the
room be with a scale of 1 inch = 2 feet?

_____   _____

The Real Number Line and Integers

EXAMPLE

$|-3| = 3$ −3 is 3 units from 0.

The absolute value of $|-3|$ is 3.

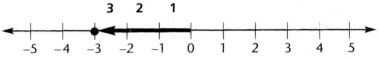

Directions   Find the absolute value.

1. $|-6|$ _____

2. $|4|$ _____

3. $|-8|$ _____

4. $|0|$ _____

5. $|11|$ _____

6. $|-72|$ _____

7. $|-31|$ _____

8. $|25|$ _____

9. $|-92|$ _____

10. $|16|$ _____

Directions   Name the opposite of each integer.

11. −6 _____

12. −9 _____

13. 15 _____

14. −24 _____

15. 11 _____

16. −52 _____

17. 84 _____

18. −5 _____

19. −42 _____

20. 38 _____

Directions   Write an integer that describes each situation.

21. The Chicago Bulls make a three-point shot in basketball. _____

22. The Green Bay Packers lose ten yards in a football game. _____

23. The stock of Company XYZ falls eight dollars in value. _____

24. School Inc., gains five dollars on the stock market. _____

25. Eighty dollars is taken out of a paycheck for taxes. _____

26. Pay fifty-five dollars for electric. _____

27. Win three hundred dollars in a raffle. _____

28. The temperature falls to twenty degrees below zero. _____

29. In five minutes, the test begins. _____

30. The test began four minutes ago. _____

Comparing Integers

Compare |–3| and 1.

|–3| is 3 units from zero, so |–3| = 3.

1 is 1 unit from zero.

3 is farther to the right than 1, so |–3| > 1.

Compare –2 and 3.

–2 is to the left of 3 on the number line.

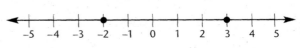

Therefore, –2 < 3.

Directions Compare each pair. Use >, <, or =.

1. –5 ☐ 1 _____
2. 11 ☐ 9 _____
3. –9 ☐ |–2| _____
4. 3 ☐ |–3| _____
5. –2 ☐ –3 _____
6. 4 ☐ –5 _____
7. –10 ☐ 3 _____
8. –2 ☐ –1 _____
9. 10 ☐ 8 _____

10. 2 ☐ –3 _____
11. 5 ☐ 6 _____
12. |–8| ☐ 6 _____
13. –6 ☐ 4 _____
14. –12 ☐ |2| _____
15. 3 ☐ –3 _____
16. 7 ☐ |–7| _____
17. |8| ☐ |–9| _____
18. 2 ☐ –1 _____

19. 2 ☐ 6 _____
20. |–6| ☐ –6 _____
21. –1 ☐ 10 _____
22. |–6| ☐ |6| _____
23. 4 ☐ 6 _____
24. –8 ☐ –9 _____
25. |–2| ☐ 2 _____

Directions Solve these problems.

26. Tuesday's temperature was –3°F. On Wednesday the temperature was –7°F. Which day was warmer?

_____

27. Draw a number line to show that |–2| is less than |–5|.

_____

28. Jimmy listed his last five golf scores for the first hole as 0, –1, 3, 1, and –2. List these scores in order from least to greatest.

_____

29. On Friday the temperature was 32°F. Saturday's temperature was 14°F. Which day was colder?

_____

30. Jamie claims –6, –2, 0, and 5 are in order from least to greatest. Is she correct?

_____

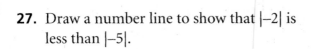

Even and Odd Integers

EXAMPLE   Find the product of 27 • 42. Tell whether it is even or odd.

27 • 42 = 1,134. This product is even, because odd • even = even.

Directions Find each sum or difference. Tell whether it is *even* or *odd*.

1. 614 − 551 _____

2. 251 − 138 _____

3. 58 + 56 _____

4. 678 − 438 _____

5. 1,235 + 15 _____

6. 89 + 381 _____

7. 216 + 429 _____

8. 368 − 122 _____

9. 128 + 147 _____

10. 791 − 543 _____

11. 360 + 369 _____

12. 192 + 189 _____

13. 372 − 276 _____

14. 2,541 + 591 _____

15. 168 − 55 _____

Directions Find each product. Tell whether it is *even* or *odd*.

16. 15 • 52 _____

17. 21 • 23 _____

18. 52 • 36 _____

19. 64 • 82 _____

20. 32 • 48 _____

21. 9 • 12 _____

22. 61 • 53 _____

23. 72 • 24 _____

24. 84 • 30 _____

25. 60 • 23 _____

26. 19 • 17 _____

27. 13 • 64 _____

28. 25 • 59 _____

29. 71 • 17 _____

30. 69 • 24 _____

Adding Positive Integers

EXAMPLE

Find the sum of –2 and 3.

Begin at –2.   Then move to the right 3 units. $-2 + 3 = 1$

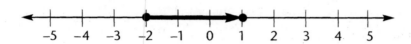

Directions Find each sum.

1. $-5 + 5$ _____

2. $4 + 7$ _____

3. $-2 + 3$ _____

4. $-9 + 9$ _____

5. $4 + 5$ _____

6. $3 + 4$ _____

7. $-8 + 2$ _____

8. $1 + 9$ _____

9. $-6 + 7$ _____

10. $7 + 8$ _____

11. $-3 + 1$ _____

12. $5 + 6$ _____

13. $-2 + 8$ _____

14. $9 + 8$ _____

15. $-5 + 7$ _____

16. $5 + 3$ _____

17. $7 + 2$ _____

18. $-9 + 7$ _____

19. $-1 + 8$ _____

20. $9 + 3$ _____

Directions Find each sum using a calculator.

21. $-251 + 787$ _____

22. $456 + 651$ _____

23. $-621 + 524$ _____

24. $876 + 957$ _____

25. $426 + 436$ _____

26. $-789 + 575$ _____

27. $-123 + 261$ _____

28. $469 + 431$ _____

29. $-921 + 951$ _____

30. $-435 + 342$ _____

Adding Negative Integers

EXAMPLE   Find the sum of 2 + (–3).

Begin at 2.   Then move to the left 3 units.   2 + (–3) = –1

$$-5 \quad -4 \quad -3 \quad -2 \quad -1 \quad 0 \quad 1 \quad 2 \quad 3 \quad 4 \quad 5$$

Directions Find each sum.

1. –5 + (–9) _____

2. 10 + (–7) _____

3. 9 + (–6) _____

4. –8 + (–3) _____

5. 1 + (–1) _____

6. –2 + (–11) _____

7. –3 + (–4) _____

8. 8 + (–5) _____

9. –7 + (–7) _____

10. 6 + (–2) _____

11. 7 + (–3) _____

12. 5 + (–8) _____

13. –1 + (–4) _____

14. –4 + (–12) _____

Directions Find each sum using a calculator.

15. –512 + (–613) _____

16. 452 + (–512) _____

17. 329 + (–144) _____

18. –482 + (–169) _____

19. 519 + (–321) _____

20. 712 + (–152) _____

21. 921 + (–671) _____

22. –159 + (–257) _____

23. –215 + (–812) _____

24. –812 + (–234) _____

25. 183 + (–161) _____

26. –821 + (–687) _____

27. 500 + (–425) _____

28. –263 + (–691) _____

Directions Solve each problem by adding integers.

29. The Brazil Basin in the Atlantic Ocean is 20,076 feet deep, which is 2,195 feet deeper than the Eurasia Basin in the Arctic Ocean. How deep is the Eurasia Basin?   _____

30. The Mariana Trench in the Pacific Ocean is 7,864 feet deeper than the Yap Trench. The Yap Trench is 27,976 feet deep. How deep is the Mariana Trench?   _____

Subtracting Positive and Negative Integers

Find the difference of $2 - (-4)$.

Begin at 2.   Then move to the right 4 units. $2 - (-4) = 6$

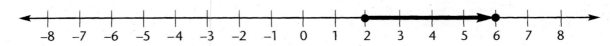

Notice that $2 - (-4) = 6$ and $2 + 4 = 6$, because subtracting -4 is the same as adding 4.

Directions   Find the sum of the new expression. (Hint: First rewrite each subtraction expression as an addition expression.)

1. $-6 - 7$ _____   **11.** $-4 - 8$ _____   **21.** $7 - 8$ _____

2. $5 - (-8)$ _____   **12.** $3 - 3$ _____   **22.** $-2 - (-4)$ _____

3. $-8 - 9$ _____   **13.** $-8 - (-8)$ _____   **23.** $4 - 5$ _____

4. $7 - (-2)$ _____   **14.** $-9 - 5$ _____   **24.** $11 - (-7)$ _____

5. $-3 - 1$ _____   **15.** $7 - 3$ _____   **25.** $-10 - 5$ _____

6. $-2 - 9$ _____   **16.** $6 - (-9)$ _____   **26.** $-9 - (-4)$ _____

7. $1 - (-6)$ _____   **17.** $-10 - 2$ _____   **27.** $5 - 3$ _____

8. $0 - 4$ _____   **18.** $6 - (-4)$ _____   **28.** $-6 - (-8)$ _____

9. $-9 - 8$ _____   **19.** $12 - (-8)$ _____

10. $5 - (-11)$ _____   **20.** $-8 - (-1)$ _____

Directions   Use integers to solve these problems.

29. The Nadelhorn, a mountain in Switzerland, is 14,196 feet. The Nadelhorn is 6,124 feet lower than Mt. McKinley in Alaska. How tall is Mt. McKinley? _____

30. Pikes Peak, Colorado, is 14,110 feet high. Mt. Kilimanjaro, Tanzania, is 5,230 feet higher. How tall is Mt. Kilimanjaro? _____

Using Positive and Negative Integers

Directions   Use the chart to find the difference in height between these points.

1. Mount Kenya and Turfan Depression

_____

2. Turfan Depression and Death Valley

_____

3. Annapurna I and Danakil Depression

_____

4. Mont Blanc and Mount McKinley

_____

5. Death Valley and Mont Blanc

_____

Highest and Lowest Points in the World	
Annapurna I, Nepal	26,504 ft
Mount McKinley, U.S.	20,320 ft
Mount Kenya, Kenya	17,058 ft
Mont Blanc, France/Italy	15,771 ft
Death Valley, U.S.	−282 ft
Danakil Depression, Ethiopia	−383 ft
Turfan Depression, China	−505 ft
Dead Sea, Israel/Jordan	−1,312 ft

Directions   Look at the chart. How many degrees separate the record high and low temperatures at these locations?

6. Seville and Roger's Pass

_____

7. Ifrane and Northice

_____

8. Vostok and El Azizia

_____

9. Rivadavia and Death Valley

_____

10. Ifrane and El Azizia

_____

Highest and Lowest Temperatures in the World	
El Azizia, Libya	136°
Death Valley, U.S.	134°
Seville, Spain	122°
Rivadavia, Argentina	120°
Ifrane, Morocco	−11°
Roger's Pass, U.S.	−70°
Northice, Greenland	−87°
Vostok, Antarctica	−129°

Multiplying by Positive Integers

EXAMPLE   Find the product (–2)(+3).

Begin at 0.   Then count by 3's to the left.   You will reach –6.   (–2)(+3) = –6

two 3's   one 3

–8   –7   –6   –5   –4   –3   –2   –1   0   1   2   3   4   5   6   7   8

Directions   Find each product.

1. (–5)(8) _____

2. (8)(6) _____

3. (–6)(7) _____

4. (3)(2) _____

5. (2)(3) _____

6. (–7)(1) _____

7. (9)(9) _____

8. (–4)(8) _____

9. (6)(8) _____

10. (–2)(9) _____

11. (5)(4) _____

12. (–1)(5) _____

13. (–9)(2) _____

14. (3)(1) _____

15. (–5)(7) _____

16. (2)(5) _____

17. (–3)(7) _____

18. (7)(6) _____

19. (–4)(9) _____

20. (1)(6) _____

Directions   Tell whether each product is *positive* or *negative*.

21. (–334)(89) _____

22. (–53)(34) _____

23. (76)(43) _____

24. (39)(643) _____

25. (–78)(28) _____

26. (675)(57) _____

27. (–522)(43) _____

28. (500)(69) _____

29. (–124)(65) _____

30. (43)(56) _____

Multiplying by Negative Integers

EXAMPLE

Find the product (–2)(–4).

The product of (–2)(–4) is +8.

When you multiply a negative number and a negative number, the product is positive.

Directions Tell whether each product is *positive* or *negative*.

1. (–52)(–45) _____

2. (56)(–432) _____

3. (34)(–33) _____

4. (–864)(–42) _____

5. (456)(–129) _____

6. (–843)(–93) _____

7. (–123)(–96) _____

8. (462)(–34) _____

9. (532)(–405) _____

10. (–831)(–100) _____

11. (800)(–52) _____

12. (–23)(–115) _____

13. (76)(–341) _____

14. (–43)(–733) _____

15. (–68)(–123) _____

16. (583)(–44) _____

17. (–346)(–721) _____

18. (57)(–33) _____

19. (–233)(–661) _____

20. (–672)(–423) _____

21. (278)(–467) _____

22. (–652)(–597) _____

23. (55)(–622) _____

24. (–18)(–577) _____

25. (457)(–24) _____

26. (–33)(–744) _____

27. (934)(–35) _____

28. (43)(–34) _____

Directions Solve each problem.

29. The temperature fell 4°F each day for six days. What was the total change in temperature? _____

30. When initially started, a commercial freezer will cool at a rate of –20°F an hour. How much colder will the freezer be in two hours? _____

Dividing Positive and Negative Integers

EXAMPLE

Find the quotient of −36 ÷ −4.

The quotient of −36 ÷ −4 is 9.

When you divide a negative number by a negative number, the quotient is positive.

Directions Find each quotient.

1. $16 \div 4$ _____

2. $(-25) \div (-5)$ _____

3. $42 \div (-6)$ _____

4. $(-30) \div 6$ _____

5. $81 \div (-9)$ _____

6. $(-20) \div 5$ _____

7. $(-18) \div 6$ _____

8. $80 \div (-10)$ _____

9. $(-14) \div 7$ _____

10. $32 \div 8$ _____

11. $(-100) \div (-25)$ _____

12. $51 \div 3$ _____

13. $(-24) \div (-6)$ _____

14. $64 \div (-8)$ _____

15. $(-28) \div 7$ _____

16. $15 \div (-5)$ _____

17. $63 \div 9$ _____

18. $(-36) \div (-6)$ _____

19. $100 \div 10$ _____

20. $(-35) \div (-7)$ _____

Directions Tell whether each quotient is *positive*, *negative*, or *zero*.

21. $453 \div (-84)$ _____

22. $0 \div 515$ _____

23. $1,256 \div (-68)$ _____

24. $(-541) \div 268$ _____

25. $4,587 \div (-67)$ _____

26. $5,532 \div 124$ _____

27. $(-5,089) \div (-301)$ _____

28. $(-854) \div 52$ _____

Directions Solve each problem.

29. A school has 704 desks. Each classroom has 32 desks. How many classrooms are in the school? _____

30. The principal of a school bought 1,000 new desks. There are 25 desks in each classroom. How many classrooms are in the school? _____

Exponents

EXAMPLE

You can use the symbol 5^3 to show $5 \bullet 5 \bullet 5$.

5^3 5 is the base. 3 is the exponent. 5^3 is read "five to the third power" or "five cubed."

When you write a negative number with an exponent, place the negative number in parentheses, and then write the exponent.

$(-6)^2$ (-6) is the base. 2 is the exponent. $(-6)^2$ is read "negative six to the second power."

m^4 m is the base. 4 is the exponent. m^4 is read "m to the fourth power."

Directions Write an expression for each phrase.

1. ten to the second power   _____
2. four to the tenth power   _____
3. negative six to the third power   _____
4. eight to the fourth power   _____
5. negative three to the second power   _____
6. two to the seventh power   _____
7. a to the fourth power   _____
8. negative ten to the fifth power   _____
9. negative b to the tenth power   _____
10. nine to the ninth power   _____

Directions Name the exponent in each of the following.

11. $(-10)^8$ _____
12. 2^9 _____
13. 5^n _____
14. 12^1 _____
15. 7^3 _____

Directions Name the base in each of the following.

16. 5^2 _____
17. 15^{10} _____
18. 2^4 _____
19. $(-5)^{11}$ _____
20. $(-n)^4$ _____

Directions Rewrite each of the following using exponents.

21. $(-7) \bullet (-7) \bullet (-7) \bullet (-7) \bullet (-7)$ _____
22. $4 \bullet 4$ _____
23. $8 \bullet 8 \bullet 8 \bullet 8$ _____
24. $(-c) \bullet (-c) \bullet (-c)$ _____
25. $12 \bullet 12 \bullet 12$ _____

Multiplying with Exponents

If two terms with exponents have the same base, you can multiply the terms by adding exponents.

$4^2 \cdot 4^3$
The base of both terms is 4.

$4^2 \cdot 4^3 = (4 \cdot 4) \cdot (4 \cdot 4 \cdot 4)$

$\qquad = 4 \cdot 4 \cdot 4 \cdot 4 \cdot 4$

$4^2 \cdot 4^3 = 4^5$

$b^2 \cdot b^2$
The base of both terms is b.

$b^2 \cdot b^2 = (b \cdot b) \cdot (b \cdot b)$

$b^2 \cdot b^2 = b^4$

$3^n \cdot 3^n$
The base of both terms is 3.

$3^n \cdot 3^n = 3^{n+n}$

$3^n \cdot 3^n = 3^{2n}$

Directions   Simplify each expression.

1. $7^4 \cdot 7^2$ 9. $3^{2y} \cdot 3^y$

2. $6^2 \cdot 6$ 10. $6^5 \cdot 6^5$

3. $(-m)^2 \cdot (-m)^8$ 11. $2^{3p} \cdot 2^{3p}$

4. $2^4 \cdot 2^3$ 12. $15^5 \cdot 15^6$

5. $n^3 \cdot n$ 13. $3^3 \cdot 3^4$

6. $14^4 \cdot 14^7$ 14. $b^3 \cdot b^3$

7. $a^5 \cdot a^2$ 15. $(-n)^2 \cdot (-n)^2$

8. $(-10)^2 \cdot (-10)^3$

Directions   Tell whether each statement is *true* or *false*. If a statement is false, tell why.

16. $(-8)^8 \cdot (-8)^8 = (-8)^{16}$ 21. $3^4 \cdot 3^2 = 3^8$

17. $5^3 \cdot 5^4 = 5^{12}$ 22. $2^6 \cdot 2^6 = 2^{12}$

18. $6^{4n} \cdot 6^{3n} = 6^{7n}$ 23. $2^n \cdot 2^{3n} = 2^{4n}$

19. $b^7 \cdot b^2 = b^5$ 24. $7^7 \cdot 7^4 = 7^{11}$

20. $25^5 \cdot 25 = 25^6$ 25. $b^2 \cdot b^{10} = b^{12}$

Dividing with Exponents

EXAMPLE   If two terms with exponents have the same base, you can divide the terms by subtracting exponents.

$8^6 \div 8^3 = \frac{8^6}{8^3}$

The base of both terms is 8.

$= \frac{(8 \cdot 8 \cdot 8 \cdot 8 \cdot 8 \cdot 8)}{(8 \cdot 8 \cdot 8)}$

$= (8 \cdot 8 \cdot 8)$

$8^6 \div 8^3 = 8^{6-3} = 8^3$

$a^4 \div a^2 = \frac{a^4}{a^2}$

$= \frac{(a \cdot a \cdot a \cdot a)}{(a \cdot a)}$

$a^4 \div a^2 = a^{4-2} = a^2$

$6^{2n} \div 6^n = \frac{6^{2n}}{6^n}$

$= \frac{(6^n \cdot 6^n)}{(6^n)}$

$6^{2n} \div 6^n = 6^{2n-n} = 6^n$

Directions Simplify each expression.

1. $7^{6n} \div 7^{3n}$ _____

2. $8^8 \div 8^2$ _____

3. $m^4 \div m^4$ _____

4. $22^8 \div 22^4$ _____

5. $k^2 \div k$ _____

6. $10^9 \div 10^7$ _____

7. $(-y)^6 \div (-y)^3$ _____

8. $11^{10} \div 11^{10}$ _____

9. $7^{14} \div 7^7$ _____

10. $10^3 \div 10$ _____

11. $(-6)^{6n} \div (-6)^{2n}$ _____

12. $2^5 \div 2^5$ _____

13. $30^4 \div 30^3$ _____

14. $d^5 \div d^2$ _____

15. $17^8 \div 17^2$ _____

Directions Tell whether each statement is *true* or *false*. If a statement is false, tell why.

16. $4^4 \div 4^4 = 4$ _____

17. $12^3 \div 12 = 12^2$ _____

18. $3^{8n} \div 3^{6n} = 3^{2n}$ _____

19. $9^7 \div 9^2 = 9^5$ _____

20. $1^5 \div 1^2 = 1^3$ _____

21. $16^4 \div 16^2 = 16^6$ _____

22. $4^6 \div 4^4 = 4^2$ _____

23. $10^{10} \div 10^3 = 10^7$ _____

24. $(-j)^7 \div (-j)^2 = (-j)^9$ _____

25. $5^{12} \div 5^2 = 5^{10}$ _____

Squares

Write an expression for the area of a square.

Area of a square = length • width = 4 • 4 = 4^2

or   Area of a square = side squared, or s^2 = 4 • 4 = 4^2

That is why 4^2 can be read as "4 squared."

Find the area of a square in square units by multiplying.

Area of a square = s^2 = 5^2

               = 5^2 = 5 • 5 = 25 sq cm

Directions Write an expression for the area of each square.

1. _____   **2.** _____   **3.** _____

Directions Multiply to find the area of each square. Use the formula Area = s^2.

4. Square with sides 7 centimeters long   _____

5. Square with sides 2 centimeters long   _____

6. Square with sides 6 centimeters long   _____

Directions Write an expression to describe the problem. Then solve the problem.

7. Alicia has a board game that is 18 inches wide and 18 inches long.
What is the area of the board game?   _____

8. Harris is cultivating a garden that is 20 feet long and 20 feet wide.
What is the area of his garden?   _____

9. The floor plan for the game room in the new recreation center is 40
feet by 40 feet. What is the floor area in the game room?   _____

10. Iris bought a new square tablecloth for the kitchen table. The cloth is 5
feet by 5 feet. What is its area?   _____

Cubes

EXAMPLE

Write an expression for the volume of a cube.

Volume = length • width • height = $2 • 2 • 2 = 2^3$

or   Volume = side cubed, or $s^3 = 2 • 2 • 2 = 2^3$

That is why 2^3 can be raed as "two cubed."

2 cm
2 cm
2 cm

Find the volume of the cube in cubic units by multiplying.

Volume = s^3

Volume = 5^3

$= 5 • 5 • 5 = 125$ cubic cm

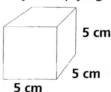
5 cm
5 cm
5 cm

Directions   Write an expression for the volume of each cube.

4
4
4

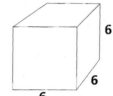
6
6
6

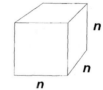
n
n
n

1. _____   2. _____   3. _____

Directions   Multiply to find the volume of each cube. Use the formula Volume = s^3.

4. Cube with sides 7 centimeters long   _____

5. Cube with sides 1 centimeter long   _____

Directions   Use a calculator to find the volume of each cube. Use the formula Volume = s^3.

6. Cube with sides 9 centimeters long   _____

7. Cube with sides 13 centimeters long   _____

8. Cube with sides 35 centimeters long   _____

Directions   Use the formula for volume to solve each problem.

9. Ana Maria keeps her hats and scarves in a decorated box with sides 8 inches long. What is the volume of the box?   _____

10. Victor's computer monitor came in a packing box with sides 3 feet long. What is the volume of the packing box?   _____

Square Roots

EXAMPLE Find the length of the side of a square.

| Area = 16 | 4 |

4

Recall that the formula for area is $A = s^2$. For this square, $A = s^2 = 4^2 = 16$.

To find the length of a side of the square, you must find the square root.

$$s = \sqrt{A} = \sqrt{16} = 4$$

EXAMPLE Find the square root of 5.

You can use a number line to estimate the square roots of numbers that are not perfect squares.

1   **2**   **3**   **4**

$1 < \ 2 < \ 3 < \ 4 < \ 5 < \ 6 < \ 7 < \ 8 < \ 9 < \ 10 < \ 11 < \ 12 < \ 13 < \ 14 < \ 15 < \ 16$

$\sqrt{1} < \sqrt{2} < \sqrt{3} < \sqrt{4} < \sqrt{5} < \sqrt{6} < \sqrt{7} < \sqrt{8} < \sqrt{9} < \sqrt{10} < \sqrt{11} < \sqrt{12} < \sqrt{13} < \sqrt{14} < \sqrt{15} < \sqrt{16}$

From the number line, you can see that $\sqrt{5}$ is between 2 and 3.

$$2 < \sqrt{5} < 3$$

To find the accurate decimal square root, use a calculator.
Round the decimal to the nearest hundredth. $\sqrt{5} = 2.24$

Directions Use the number line to make each statement true. Then use a calculator to find a decimal value of each square root. Round the decimal to the nearest hundredth.

1. $\Box < \sqrt{15} < \Box$ _____

2. $\Box < \sqrt{12} < \Box$ _____

3. $\Box < \sqrt{8} < \Box$ _____

4. $\Box < \sqrt{11} < \Box$ _____

5. $\Box < \sqrt{3} < \Box$ _____

6. $\Box < \sqrt{7} < \Box$ _____

7. $\Box < \sqrt{14} < \Box$ _____

8. $\Box < \sqrt{6} < \Box$ _____

Directions Find the length of a side of the square. You may use your calculator. Round to the nearest hundredth if necessary.

9. Area = 25 _____

10. Area = 39 _____

Irrational Numbers and Square Roots

EXAMPLE

The square roots of some numbers are whole numbers. Whole numbers are rational numbers. For example, $\sqrt{25} = 5$, which is a whole number and is a rational number.

The square roots of some numbers are not whole numbers. They are irrational numbers. For example, $\sqrt{3} = 1.73$, which is not a whole number and is an irrational number.

You can use a graph to find the approximate value of an irrational number.

Find the value of $\sqrt{50}$ on the graph below.

Step 1 Estimate the value of $\sqrt{50}$. 50 is between the perfect squares 49 and 64, so $\sqrt{50}$ is between 7 and 8.

Step 2 Find 50 on the left-hand scale and draw a straight line to the graph.

Step 3 Draw a straight line from the point of the graph to the bottom axis. That line will cross the axis at about $\sqrt{50}$. The value is about 7.1.

Step 4 Compare your estimated value to the calculator value, which is 7.07. So 7.1 for the graph is close to the calculator value of 7.07 rounded to the nearest hundredth.

Directions Use the graph to estimate these values.

1. $\sqrt{95}$ _____

2. $\sqrt{90}$ _____

3. $\sqrt{85}$ _____

4. $\sqrt{80}$ _____

5. $\sqrt{75}$ _____

6. $\sqrt{70}$ _____

7. $\sqrt{65}$ _____

8. $\sqrt{60}$ _____

9. $\sqrt{45}$ _____

10. $\sqrt{40}$ _____

11. $\sqrt{35}$ _____

12. $\sqrt{30}$ _____

13. $\sqrt{25}$ _____

14. $\sqrt{20}$ _____

15. $\sqrt{15}$ _____

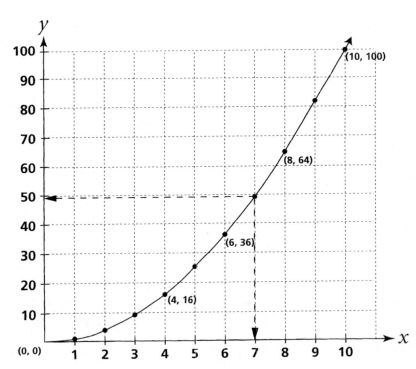

Irrational Numbers as Decimals

EXAMPLE   Find each root. Tell whether it is *rational* or *irrational*.

$\sqrt{3}$

Using a calculator: $\sqrt{3}$ = 1.73205...

The number is *irrational* because it neither ends in zeroes nor has a repeating pattern.

$\sqrt[3]{27}$

Using a calculator: $\sqrt[3]{27}$ = 3.0

The number is *rational* because it ends in zeroes.

Directions Complete the chart. Find each root and tell whether it is *rational* or *irrational*. You may use a calculator.

Radical	Root	Rational or Irrational?
$\sqrt{49}$	1. _____	2. _____
$\sqrt{15}$	3. _____	4. _____
$\sqrt{11}$	5. _____	6. _____
$\sqrt{6}$	7. _____	8. _____
$\sqrt{144}$	9. _____	10. _____
$\sqrt{121}$	11. _____	12. _____
$\sqrt{50}$	13. _____	14. _____
$\sqrt[3]{50}$	15. _____	16. _____
$\sqrt{36}$	17. _____	18. _____
$\sqrt[3]{18}$	19. _____	20. _____
$\sqrt{169}$	21. _____	22. _____
$\sqrt[3]{125}$	23. _____	24. _____

Directions Solve the problem.

25. Caitlin has cut out a square piece of graph paper that contains a total of 81 blocks. How many blocks are there along one side of the square?

_____

Radicals in Equations

EXAMPLE   Solve for *x*: $\sqrt{x} + 2 = 13$

Step 1 Isolate the variable, *x*. $\sqrt{x} + 2 - 2 = 13 - 2$

$\sqrt{x} = 11$

Step 2 Square both sides. $(\sqrt{x})^2 = 11^2$

$x = 121$

Step 3 Check. $\sqrt{121} + 2 = 13$

$11 + 2 = 13 \qquad 13 = 13$

True

Directions Solve each equation for the variable. Check your answers.

1. $\sqrt{x} = 5$ _____

2. $\sqrt{n} = 8$ _____

3. $\sqrt{k + 3} = 2$ _____

4. $\sqrt{a} = 13$ _____

5. $\sqrt{r + 8} = 12$ _____

6. $\sqrt{y - 5} = 5$ _____

7. $\sqrt{m} = 16$ _____

8. $\sqrt{4n - 3} = 3$ _____

Directions Solve the problems. Show the equation as well as your answer.

9. Kristen challenges you with this puzzle: "Add the square root of a mystery number to the square root of 100. The result is 19. What is the mystery number?"

_____

10. Jaime buys a square tablecloth. The package label declares, "The area of this tablecloth is 800 square inches." What is the length of a side of the cloth? (Express your answer as a simplified radical.)

_____

The Pythagorean Theorem

EXAMPLE

In any right triangle, sides *a* and *b* are the sides of the triangle that form the right angle. Side *c* is the hypotenuse, or longest side, of a right triangle. If you know the length of two sides of a right triangle, you can use the Pythagorean theorem to find the length of the third side.

The Pythagorean theorem is this formula: $a^2 + b^2 = c^2$.

Use the Pythagorean theorem to find the hypotenuse of this right triangle.

Step 1 Substitute the values in the equation. Then square the values.

$$c^2 = a^2 + b^2$$

$$c^2 = 6^2 + 8^2$$

$$c^2 = 36 + 64$$

Step 2 Take the square root of each side of the equation.

$$\sqrt{c^2} = \sqrt{36 + 64}$$

$$c = \sqrt{100}$$

$$c = 10$$

The hypotenuse is 10 units long.

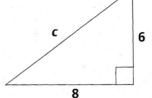

Directions Use the Pythagorean theorem to find the length of the side not given. You may use a calculator. If necessary, round to the nearest tenth.

1. _____

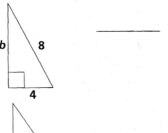

2. _____

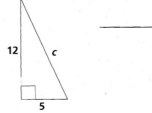

3. _____

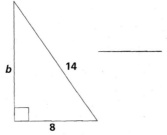

4. _____

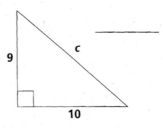

5. _____

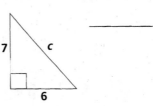

More About Triangles

EXAMPLE

Is this scalene triangle a right triangle?

Step 1 Write the Pythagorean formula.

$a^2 + b^2 = c^2$

Step 2 Substitute the triangle's values for a, b, and c.

$a^2 + b^2 = c^2$

$6^2 + 8^2 = 10^2$

$36 + 64 = 100$

The equation is true, so this scalene triangle is also a right triangle.

Directions Answer the question. Then use the Pythagorean theorem to determine whether the triangle is also a right triangle.

1. Is this triangle a scalene triangle, an isosceles triangle, or an equilateral triangle?

_____ Is it a right triangle? _____

2. Is this triangle a scalene triangle, an isosceles triangle, or an equilateral triangle?

_____ Is it a right triangle? _____

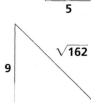

3. Is this triangle a scalene triangle, an isosceles triangle, or an equilateral triangle?

_____ Is it a right triangle? _____

4. Is this triangle a scalene triangle, an isosceles triangle, or an equilateral triangle?

_____ Is it a right triangle? _____

5. Is this triangle a scalene triangle, an isosceles triangle, or an equilateral triangle?

_____ Is it a right triangle? _____

Mathematics: Pathways

Perimeters of Polygons

EXAMPLE Find the perimeter of this figure.

Perimeter = 5 + 6 + 8 = 19 cm

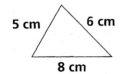

5 cm   6 cm

8 cm

Directions Find the perimeter of each figure.

1.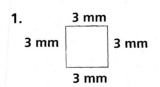

3 mm

3 mm   3 mm

3 mm

_____

2.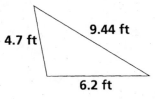

4.7 ft   9.44 ft

6.2 ft

_____

3. 3 yd

$2\frac{1}{2}$ yd $2\frac{1}{2}$ yd

3 yd

_____

4.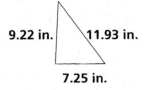

9.22 in.   11.93 in.

7.25 in.

_____

Directions Solve each problem to find the perimeter.

5. The sides of a quadrilateral measure $6\frac{7}{8}$ ft, $4\frac{1}{2}$ ft, $3\frac{1}{8}$ ft, and $7\frac{1}{2}$ ft. What is the perimeter? _____

6. Two sides of an isosceles triangle measure 6.42 m each. The remaining side measures 9.73 m. What is the perimeter of the triangle? _____

7. Each side of an equilateral triangle measures 48 yards. What is the perimeter? _____

8. A scalene triangle has sides measuring 532.6 ft, 429.3 ft, and 830.6 ft. What is the perimeter? _____

Directions Solve each problem.

9. Hector made a dog kennel in his backyard. He used a total of 28 feet of fencing, including the gate. If two sides of the kennel are ten feet each, what are the lengths of the other two sides? _____

10. Maya has 13.75 inches of gold string, which she wants to glue around a picture frame in the shape of an equilateral triangle. Each side of the triangle is 4.25 inches. Does she have enough string? _____

Perimeters of Regular Polygons

EXAMPLE Each side of a regular pentagon measures
6.9 cm. Find the perimeter.

$P = 5(6.9) = 34.5$ cm

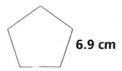

6.9 cm

Directions Find the perimeter of each regular polygon.

1.

8 ft

_____

2.
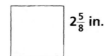
$2\frac{5}{8}$ in.

_____

3.
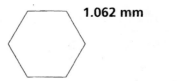
1.062 mm

_____

4.
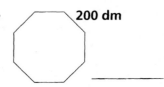
200 dm

_____

5.
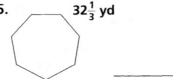
$32\frac{1}{3}$ yd

_____

6.
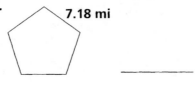
7.18 mi

_____

Directions Find the number of sides that each shape has.

7. Each side of a regular polygon measures 3.67 m. The perimeter of the
    polygon is 47.71 m. How many sides does this regular polygon have?

    _____

8. The perimeter of a regular polygon is 1,071 cm. Each side of the
    polygon measures 63 cm. How many sides does this regular polygon
    have?

    _____

9. The sum of all sides of a regular polygon is 253 ft. Each side measures
    11 ft. How many sides does this regular polygon have?

    _____

10. The perimeter of a regular polygon is 13.125 ft. Each side measures
    1.875 ft. How many sides does this regular polygon have?

    _____

Perimeters of Irregular Polygons

Find the perimeter of this polygon.

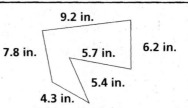

9.2 in.

7.8 in.   5.7 in.   6.2 in.

5.4 in.

4.3 in.

$P = 6.2 + 5.7 + 5.4 + 4.3 + 7.8 + 9.2 = 38.6$ in.

Directions Find the perimeter of each polygon.

1.

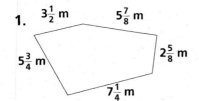

$3\frac{1}{2}$ m $5\frac{7}{8}$ m

$5\frac{3}{4}$ m $2\frac{5}{8}$ m

$7\frac{1}{4}$ m

_____

2.

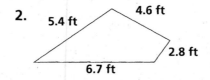

5.4 ft   4.6 ft

2.8 ft

6.7 ft

_____

3.

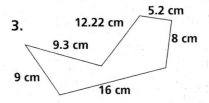

5.2 cm

12.22 cm

8 cm

9.3 cm

9 cm   16 cm

_____

4.

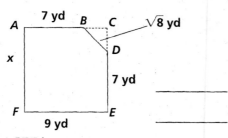

23 mm   15 mm

19.5 mm

58.5 mm

32 mm

46.7 mm

_____

5.

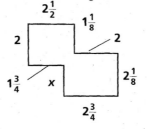

$9\frac{2}{3}$ yd

5 yd $8\frac{3}{4}$ yd

9 yd

_____

6.

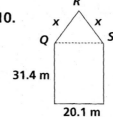

12.5 in.   13.6 in.

15.2 in.

8 in.

28 in.

22 in.

_____

Directions Find the measure of each missing x. Then find the perimeter of each polygon.

7.

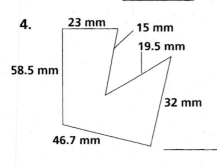

17

2

10

3

x

14

_____

_____

8.

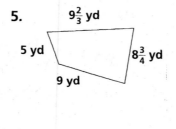

$2\frac{1}{2}$

$1\frac{1}{8}$

2   2

$1\frac{3}{4}$ x $2\frac{1}{8}$

$2\frac{3}{4}$

_____

_____

9.

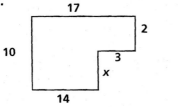

7 yd

A   B   C $\sqrt{8}$ yd

x D

7 yd

F   E

9 yd

_____

_____

ACEF is a square.

10.

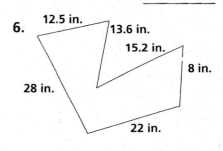

R

x x

Q   S

31.4 m

20.1 m

_____

_____

Triangle *QRS* is an equilateral triangle.

Areas of Rectangles and Squares

EXAMPLE   Find the area of square *LMNO*.

Substitute 5.2 into the formula $A = s^2$.

$A = (5.2)^2 = 27.04$ in.^{2}

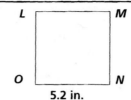

5.2 in.

Directions Find the area of each rectangle.

1. Rectangle with $l = 8$ ft and $w = 6$ ft   _____

2. Rectangle with $l = 13$ m and $w = 4$ m   _____

3. Rectangle with $l = 15.5$ cm and $w = 8$ cm   _____

4. Rectangle with $l = 4\frac{1}{2}$ yd and $w = 6\frac{1}{4}$ yd   _____

Directions Find the area of each square.

5. Square with $s = 10$ mm _____   7. Square with $s = 4.2$ cm _____

6. Square with $s = 21$ ft   _____   8. Square with $s = 5\frac{1}{2}$ m _____

Directions Use the formula $A = s^2$ and a calculator to find the area of each square.

9. $s = 23$ m _____   11. $s = 8.5$ cm _____   13. $s = 1.42$ mi _____

10. $s = 6.7$ ft _____   12. $s = 42$ in. _____

Directions Solve each problem.

14. Allen is painting a family room. Two walls are 8 ft high and 15 ft long. The other two walls are 8 ft high and 9 ft long. Allen has one gallon of paint, which will cover 400 ft^2 of walls. Will he have enough paint? Explain.

_____

15. Consuela cuts lawns as a part-time job. The last lawn she cut was rectangular and totaled 1,365 yd^2. One side of the lawn was 35 yards long. What was the length of the other side?

_____

Areas of Triangles

EXAMPLE Find the area of triangle *XYZ*.

Use the formula $A = \frac{1}{2}bh$.

$A = \frac{1}{2}(6)(10)$

$A = \frac{1}{2}(60)$

$A = 30 \text{ m}^2$

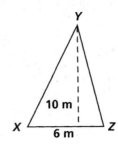

Directions Find the area of each figure.

1.

6 ft
4 ft

_____

2.

15 m
12 m

_____

3.

16 km
9 km

_____

Directions Find the base or height of each triangle.

4. The area of a triangle is 12 ft^2 and the base is 4 ft. What is the height? _____

5. The area of a triangle is 32 in.^{2} and the height is 8 in. What is the base? _____

6. The area of a triangle is 15 m^2 and the base is 10 m. What is the height? _____

7. The area of a triangle is 36 yd^2 and the height is 9 yd. What is the base? _____

8. The area of a triangle is 36 km^2 and the height is 12 km. What is the base? _____

Directions Solve these problems.

9. Howard is constructing a triangular garden edge out of brick. The base of the garden is 15 ft. The area is 165 ft^2. What is the height of the triangle?

_____

10. Jana is making curtains in the shape of triangles. She needs to make two triangle curtains for one window. The triangles have a base of 2 ft and a height of 4 ft. What is the total area of the triangle curtains for one window?

_____

Areas of Trapezoids and Parallelograms

Find the area of trapezoid *STRU*.

$$A = \frac{b_1 + b_2}{2}h$$

$$A = \frac{6 + 20}{2}(10) = \frac{26}{2}(10)$$

$$A = (13)(10) = 130 \text{ m}^2$$

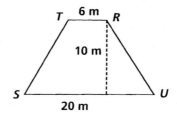

Directions Find the area of each quadrilateral.

1.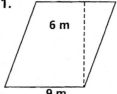

6 m

9 m _____

2.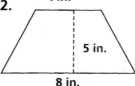

4 in.

5 in.

8 in. _____

3.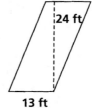

24 ft

13 ft _____

Directions Find the base or height of each quadrilateral.

4. A parallelogram has a height of 9 cm and an area of 108 cm².

   What is the length of its base? _____

5. A trapezoid has one base 6 ft long and another base 8 ft long. Its area is 240 ft².

   What is its height? _____

6. If a parallelogram has a base of 11 m and an area of 176 m², what is its height?

   _____

7. A parallelogram has a height of 12 in. and an area of 168 in.².

   What is the length of its base? _____

8. The bases of a trapezoid equal 16 km and its area is 32 km². What is its height? _____

9. If a parallelogram has a base of 13 mm and an area of 78 mm²,

   what is its height? _____

10. The bases of a trapezoid equal 17 yd and its area is 68 yd². What is its height? _____

Areas of Irregular Polygons

EXAMPLE   Find the area of this polygon.

Divide the polygon into smaller regions to calculate the areas.

$A = (5 \bullet 7) + (2 \bullet 3)$

$A = 35 + 6 = 41$ units^2

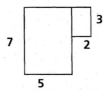

Directions   Find the area of each polygon.

1.

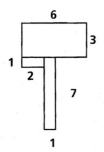

_____

2.

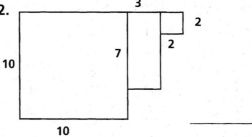

_____

3.

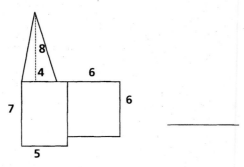

_____

4.

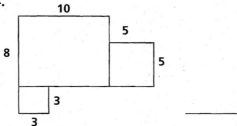

_____

5.

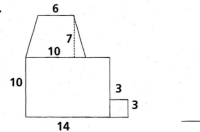

_____

Working with Areas of Shapes

Directions Find the area of each rectangle or square.

1. Rectangle with $l = 9$ in. and $w = 3.85$ in.   _____

2. Rectangle with $l = 3\frac{1}{3}$ mi and $w = 7\frac{1}{2}$ mi   _____

3. Square with $s = 16.3$ yd   _____

4. Square with $s = 3\frac{1}{4}$ ft   _____

5. Square with $s = 12.33$ mi   _____

Directions Use the area to find the base or height of each triangle, trapezoid, or parallelogram.

6. The area of a triangle is 14 ft^2 and the base is 7 ft. What is the height?   _____

7. The area of a triangle is 15 mm^2 and the height is 5 mm. What is the base?   _____

8. The area of a triangle is 9 cm^2 and the base is 3 cm. What is the height?   _____

9. The area of a triangle is 50 in.^{2} and the base is 10 in. What is the height?   _____

10. The area of a triangle is 80 m^2 and the height is 8 m. What is the base?   _____

11. The area of a triangle is 40.5 ft^2 and the base is 9 ft. What is the height?   _____

12. The area of a triangle is 17.5 dm^2 and the height is 7 dm. What is the base?   _____

13. A trapezoid has one base 23 in. long and another base 27 in. long. Its area is 400 in.^{2}.

    What is its height? _____

14. The bases of a trapezoid equal 68 mm and its area is 1,768 mm^2.

    What is its height? _____

15. A parallelogram has a height of 23 mi and an area of 667 mi^2.

    What is the length of its base? _____

Circumferences and Areas of Circles

EXAMPLE
Find the circumference and area of a circle with a radius of 5 feet.
To find the circumference, use the formula $C = \pi d$.
First, calculate the diameter.
$2 \cdot 5 = 10$ feet
$C = (3.14)(10) = 31.4$ feet
To find the area, use the formula $A = \pi r^2$.
$A = (3.14)(5^2) = 78.5$ feet^2

Directions Find the circumference of a circle with the given radius or diameter. Use the formula $C = \pi d$. Use 3.14 for π.

1. radius = 4 in. _____

2. diameter = 6 ft _____

3. radius = 2 m _____

4. diameter = 10 mm _____

5. radius = 7 km _____

Directions Find the area of a circle with the given radius or diameter. Use the formula $A = \pi r^2$. Use 3.14 for π.

6. radius = 3 yd _____

7. diameter = 10 cm _____

8. radius = 7 ft _____

9. diameter = 4 m _____

10. diameter = 14 in. _____

11. radius = 6 km _____

12. radius = 5 mi _____

13. diameter = 6 in. _____

14. radius = 8 ft _____

15. radius = 10 m _____

Directions Use a calculator and the formula $A = \pi r^2$ to find the areas of circles with the following measures. Use 3.14 for π.

16. diameter = 1.25 yd _____

17. radius = 215 mi _____

18. radius = 6.7 ft _____

19. diameter = 9.5 m _____

20. radius = 1.8 km _____

Solid Figures

EXAMPLE   Name the shape. Mark each face with an arrow, and count the number of faces found.

     Step 1   Name the shape.

              Cube

     Step 2   Count the number of faces on the shape.

              The cube has six faces.

Directions   Name the shape, and look for either edges or vertices. Write the number of edges or vertices found.

1. _____

         _____ edges

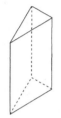

3. _____

         _____ vertices

2. _____

         _____ edges

4. _____

         _____ vertices

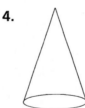

Directions   Name the shape. Write how many faces, edges, and vertices the shape has.

5. _____

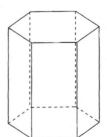

         _____ faces

         _____ edges

         _____ vertices

Surface Areas of Prisms and Cylinders

EXAMPLE The formula for the surface area of a rectangular prism is

$$SA = 2(lw + hl + hw).$$

You are given values of 5, 7, and 6 for *l, w,* and *h.*

Write the equation $SA = 2((5 \cdot 7)+(5 \cdot 6)+(6 \cdot 7))$. This can be reduced to $SA = 2(35 + 30 + 42) = 2(107) = 214.$

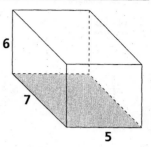

Directions Find the surface area of each of the following three-dimensional figures. Round your answer to the nearest hundredth.

1.

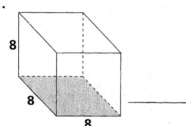

2.

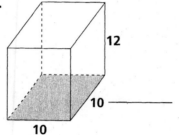

3.

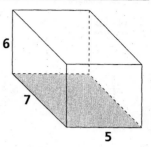

4.

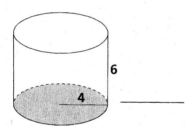

5.

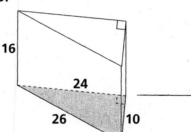

6.

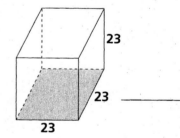

7.

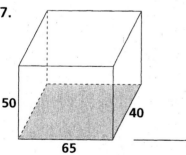

8.

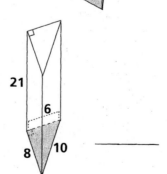

9.

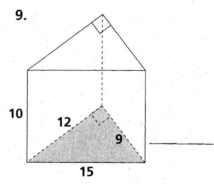

10.

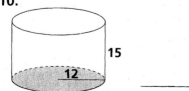

Surface Areas of Pyramids and Cones

Find the surface area of this pyramid. The formula for the surface area of a pyramid is SA = area of base + area of four triangles.

$$SA = (s \cdot s) + \tfrac{1}{2}sl + \tfrac{1}{2}sl + \tfrac{1}{2}sl + \tfrac{1}{2}sl = s^2 + 2sl \text{ where}$$
l is the measure of the slant height.

You are given a value of 15 for s and a value of 10 for l.

Write the equation $SA = 15^2 + 2(15 \cdot 10)$.

This can be simplified to $SA = 225 + 300 = 525$.

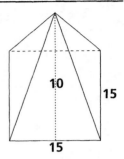

Directions Find the surface area of these pyramids and cones. Round your answer to the nearest hundredth.

1.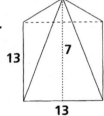
13   7
13
_____

2.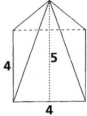
7
4
_____

3.
4   5
4
_____

4.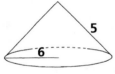
5
6
_____

5.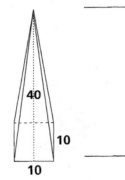
40
10
10
_____

6.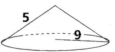
5
9
_____

7.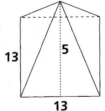
13   5
13
_____

8.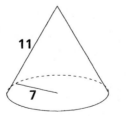
11
7
_____

9.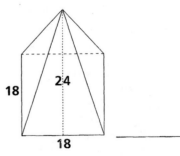
18   24
18
_____

10.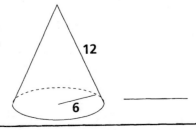
12
6
_____

Volumes of Cubes, Prisms, and Pyramids

Find the volume of this rectangular prism.

$V = lwh$

$V = (7)(5)(4) = 140$ in.^{3}

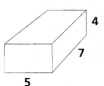

Directions   Find the volume of each figure.

1.

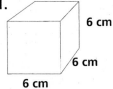

6 cm

6 cm

6 cm

2.

3 ft

6 ft

4 ft

3.

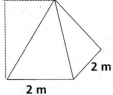

6 m

2 m

2 m

Directions   Use the formula $V = e^3$ and a calculator to find the volume of each cube.

4. $e = 23$ mm   _____

5. $e = 1.8$ in.   _____

6. $e = 126$ ft   _____

7. $e = 0.9$ mi   _____

8. $e = 50$ cm   _____

9. $e = 1.02$ km   _____

10. $e = 68$ dm   _____

11. $e = 43$ m   _____

12. $e = 19.2$ in.   _____

13. $e = 202$ ft   _____

Directions   Solve each problem.

14. Marcus is shipping books to his brother in New York. The box is 10 inches by 10 inches and 6 inches deep. Each book is 5 inches by 5 inches and 2 inches thick. How many books can Marcus ship in one package?

_____

15. Lisa's suitcase is 18 inches wide, 32 inches high, and 36 inches long. What is the volume of the suitcase?

_____

Volumes of Cylinders, Cones, and Spheres

EXAMPLE   Find the volume of this cylinder.

Use the formula $V = \pi r^2 h$.

$V = (3.14)(6)^2(10) = (3.14)(36)(10)$

$V = 1,130.4 \text{ in.}^3$

10 in.

6 in.

Directions   Find the volume of a cylinder with the given height and radius or diameter. Use the formula $V = \pi r^2 h$. Use 3.14 for π.

1. diameter = 6 in.; height = 5 in.   _____   4. radius = 3 cm; height = 2 cm   _____

2. radius = 4 ft; height = 7 ft   _____   5. diameter = 2 yd; height = 6 yd   _____

3. diameter = 10 mm; height = 8 mm _____   6. diameter = 4 cm; height = 4 cm   _____

Directions   Find the volume of a cone with the given height and radius or diameter. Use the formula $V = \frac{1}{3}\pi r^2 h$. Use 3.14 for π.

7. radius = 9 m; height = 13 m   _____   10. diameter = 6 yd; height = 50 yd   _____

8. radius = 1 ft; height = 6 ft   _____   11. diameter = 9 m; height = 1.5 m   _____

9. radius = 7 cm; height = 14 cm   _____   12. diameter = 25 mm; height = 11 mm _____

Directions   Find the volume of a sphere with the given radius or diameter. Use the formula $V = \frac{4}{3}\pi r^3$. Use 3.14 for π.

13. radius = 3 cm   _____   16. diameter = 30 cm   _____

14. radius = 6 ft   _____   17. radius = 12 ft   _____

15. diameter = 48 mm   _____   18. diameter = 21 m   _____

Directions   Solve each problem.

19. George filled a plastic bag with water until it had a diameter of 9 inches.
    What was the volume of the bag?   _____

20. Lin has two boxes to choose from to mail a package to her sister in Florida.
    One is a rectangular box measuring 12 inches long, 9 inches high, and
    10 inches wide. The other is a cylinder with a diameter of 10 inches and a height
    of 14 inches. She wants the larger box. Which one should she pick? Explain.

_____

Graphing Equalities

EXAMPLE

Graph the solution $x = -3$ on a number line.

Step 1 Draw a number line.

Step 2 Make a shaded circle on the number line at -3.

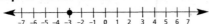

Directions Graph each solution on a number line.

1. $t = 5$ **5.** $y = -3$ **9.** $s = -\frac{1}{3}$

2. $a = 3$ **6.** $q = -10$ **10.** $m = 2$

3. $d = -5$ **7.** $j = 6$

4. $x = 0$ **8.** $z = -2$

Directions Write a solution for each equality. Use x as the variable in each of the solutions.

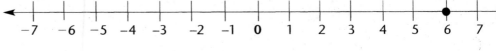

11. _____

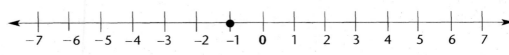

12. _____

13. _____

14. _____

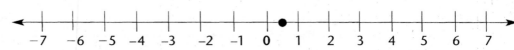

15. _____

Graphing Inequalities

EXAMPLE

Graph the solution $y > 1$ on a number line.

Step 1 Draw a number line.

Step 2 Note that $y > 1$ means the solution is greater than 1.

Step 3 Make an open circle on 1 with a line extending right and an arrow pointing right.

Directions Graph each solution on a number line.

1. $y > 8$ 5. $a \geq 6$ 9. $l \neq 8$

2. $x < 4$ 6. $w < -5$ 10. $k \geq -3$

3. $t \leq -2$ 7. $h > -9$

4. $s > 0$ 8. $j \leq 12$

Directions Write a solution for each inequality. Use x as the variable in each of the solutions.

11. _____

12. _____

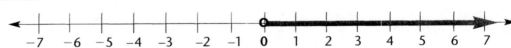

13. _____

14. _____

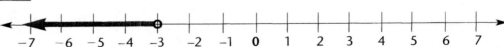

15. _____

Name_____ Date_____ Period_____

Graphing Solutions of Equalities

EXAMPLE   Solve $c + 4 = 10$ for c. Then graph the solution.

Step 1 Solve for c by subtracting 4 from each side of the equality.

$c + 4 - 4 = 10 - 4$ $c = 10 - 4$ $c = 6$

Step 2 Graph the solution on a number line.

Step 3 Check your work by substitution.

$c + 4 = 10$ $6 + 4 = 10$ True

Directions Solve each equality for the variable. Then graph and check each solution.

1. $x + 3 = 7$ _____

2. $5 + c = 4$ _____

3. $h - 3 = 0$ _____

4. $m + 6 = -3$ _____

5. $4 + j = -1$ _____

6. $s - 2 = 4$ _____

7. $g + 7 = 3$ _____

8. $7 + v = 9$ _____

9. $d - 1 = 7$ _____

10. $p - 3 = -5$ _____

11. $y + 5 = -3$ _____

12. $t - 7 = -6$ _____

13. $a + 9 = 9$ _____

14. $e - 8 = 5$ _____

15. $l - 2 = 3$ _____

16. $b + 10 = -5$ _____

17. $-5 + n = -3$ _____

18. $z - 3 = 4$ _____

Directions Write and solve an equality for each problem. Use x as the variable in the equality. Graph your solution on a number line.

19. Calvin sprinted 300 meters more today than yesterday. He sprinted 900 meters today. How many meters did he sprint yesterday?   _____

20. Maria jumped 3 inches farther in the long jump Thursday than Friday. She jumped 6 feet 8 inches on Friday. How far did she jump on Thursday?   _____

Graphing Solutions of Inequalities

EXAMPLE Solve $m + 3 \leq 10$ for m. Then graph the solution.

Step 1 Solve for m by subtracting 3 from each side of the inequality.

$m + 3 - 3 \leq 10 - 3 \qquad m \leq 7$

Step 2 Graph the solution on a number line.

Step 3 Check your work by substitution.

$7 + 3 \leq 10 \qquad 10 \leq 10 \qquad$ True

Directions Solve each equality or inequality for the variable. Then graph and check each solution.

1. $x + 4 \leq 6$ _____

2. $p - 3 < 8$ _____

3. $2 + d > -2$ _____

4. $t - 2 > -4$ _____

5. $r - 6 \geq -1$ _____

6. $e + 3 < -4$ _____

7. $w - 5 \leq 6$ _____

8. $q + 5 \leq 2$ _____

9. $a - 7 < 2$ _____

10. $b - 1 > -3$ _____

11. $x + 4 < -6$ _____

12. $2 + f \geq -4$ _____

13. $s - 9 > -6$ _____

14. $g + 7 \geq 9$ _____

15. $n - 8 \leq -5$ _____

16. $m - 2 \geq 8$ _____

17. $k + 8 < 7$ _____

18. $p - 6 > 5$ _____

19. $w + 2 \leq -1$ _____

20. $4 + u > 8$ _____

21. $d - 7 < -5$ _____

22. $i - 4 \geq 1$ _____

23. $-1 + z \geq 0$ _____

Directions Write and solve an inequality for each problem. Use x as the variable in the inequality. Graph your solution on a number line.

24. The results of a survey taken at Washington High School showed that 6 or fewer of every 10 people said rock music was their favorite type of music. How many people did not choose rock music?

_____

25. The number of students attending a home basketball game at Washington High School is always at least 25 more than the number of rows in the bleachers. There are 10 rows of bleachers. How many people attend each home game?

_____

The Coordinate System—Locating Points

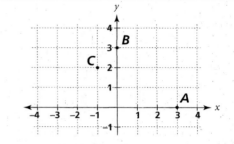

EXAMPLE

Locate points *A*, *B*, and *C*. Remember to always read the *x*-axis first, then the *y*-axis.

The ordered pair for Point *A* is (3, 0).

The ordered pair for Point *B* is (0, 3).

The ordered pair for Point *C* is (−1, 2).

Directions Write the ordered pair that describes the location of each point.

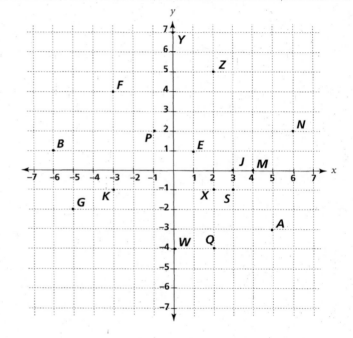

1. Point *E* _____

2. Point *J* _____

3. Point *K* _____

4. Point *N* _____

5. Point *P* _____

6. Point *Q* _____

7. Point *Y* _____

8. Point *B* _____

9. Point *F* _____

10. Point *W* _____

11. Point *M* _____

12. Point *X* _____

13. Point *A* _____

14. Point *G* _____

15. Point *Z* _____

Directions Identify the quadrant in which each of these points is located.

16. Point *N* _____

17. Point *A* _____

18. Point *B* _____

19. Point *G* _____

20. Point *Z* _____

The Coordinate System—Plotting Points

EXAMPLE

Plot a point at (–3, 2). Label the point C.

Step 1 Construct a coordinate system large enough to include the ordered pair (–3, 2).

Step 2 To plot (–3, 2), begin at the origin (0,0). Move 3 units *left* on the *x*-axis.

Step 3 Move 2 units up.

Step 4 Make a shaded circle at (–3, 2).

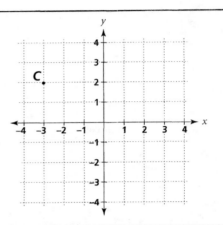

Directions On a sheet of graph paper, draw a coordinate system. Then use it to plot and label each point shown in problems 1–20.

1. Point X (5, 6)

2. Point Q (2, –5)

3. Point A (–5, 0)

4. Point W (–1, –3)

5. Point S (–2, 5)

6. Point Z (1, 3)

7. Point E (–4, 6)

8. Point D (3, –4)

9. Point C (–5, –4)

10. Point V (0, 6)

11. Point F (–6, –3)

12. Point R (–7, 5)

13. Point T (5, –5)

14. Point G (4, 6)

15. Point B (–1, 5)

16. Point Y (–7, –8)

17. Point H (–6, –7)

18. Point N (7, –6)

19. Point J (4, 4)

20. Point M (2, –6)

Directions Using the above points, identify the quadrant in which each point is located.

21. Point F _____

22. Point N _____

23. Point G _____

24. Point B _____

25. Point Q _____

Determining the Points of a Line

EXAMPLE

Complete the table of values for the line $y = x + 3$.

Step 1 Substitute –2 for x and solve for y.

$y = x + 3$ $y = -2 + 3$ $y = 1$

Step 2 Substitute 3 for y and solve for x.

$y = x + 3$ $3 = x + 3$ $3 - 3 = x + 3 - 3$ $0 = x$

Step 3 Substitute 4 for x and solve for y.

$y = x + 3$ $y = 4 + 3$ $y = 7$

Step 4 Complete the table of values.

$y = x + 3$	
x	y
–2	
	3
4	

$y = x + 3$	
x	y
–2	1
0	3
4	7

Directions Complete each table of values.

1.

$y = x + 5$	
x	y
–3	
2	
6	

2.

$y = x - 4$	
x	y
–2	
–1	
	–1

3.

$y = x + 7$	
x	y
–4	
	7
4	

4.

$y = x - 3$	
x	y
	1
	–3
	–5

5.

$y = x + 9$	
x	y
	6
	9
5	

6.

$y = x + 8$	
x	y
	1
0	
	10

7.

$y = x - 2$	
x	y
–1	
	1
	4

8.

$y = x + 6$	
x	y
–7	
	2
–1	

Directions Use a calculator to complete the tables of values.

9.

$y = x + 25.7$	
x	y
	18.8
–3.4	
8.7	

10.

$y = x - 12.3$	
x	y
–7.8	
	–8.2
	10.9

Tables of Values and Coordinate Systems

Directions Make a table of values for each linear equation.

1.

$y = x + 1$	
x	y

2.

$y = x - 5$	
x	y

3.

$y = x - 7$	
x	y

4.

$y = x - 1$	
x	y

5.

$y = x + 2$	
x	y

6.

$y = x + 4$	
x	y

Directions On a sheet of graph paper, draw a coordinate system with x values from −7 to 7 and y values from −7 to 7. Suppose that the system stands for a grid to map a lake. Use it to answer these questions.

7. How far away is the sandbar (2, 0) from the boat (2, 6)?

_____

8. Willie drives the boat (2, 6) to the sandbar (2, 0) and then to the deepest part of the lake (−4, 0). How far does he drive the boat?

_____

9. Sarah swims from the end of the sandbar (−1, 0) to the boat dock (−1, −7). How far does she swim?

_____

10. Zach walks along the sandbar (2, 0) to the end of the sandbar (−1, 0) and back again. How far does he walk?

_____

Lines as Functions

EXAMPLE   A function is a rule that associates every *x*-value with one and only one *y*-value. If a vertical line crosses a graph more than once, the graph is *not* a function.

- A *circle* is *not* a function. A vertical line will cross it at two points.

- A *straight line* is a function. A vertical line crosses it at one point only.

Directions   Is each graph an example of a function? Write *yes* or *no*. Explain your answer.

1. _____
   _____
   _____

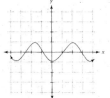

2. _____
   _____
   _____

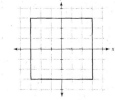

3. _____
   _____
   _____

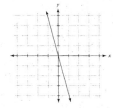

4. _____
   _____
   _____

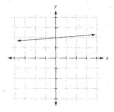

5. _____
   _____
   _____

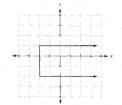

Domain and Range of a Function

EXAMPLE Find the range of the function $y = f(x) = 3x + 1$ for the domain –2, 0, 3, 6
Substitute the domain values in $f(x)$

$x = -2$ $y = f(-2) = 3(-2) + 1 = -5$ so $y = -5$ $x = 3$ $y = f(3) = 3(3) + 1 = 10$ so $y = 10$

$x = 0$ $y = f(0) = 3(0) + 1 = 1$ so $y = 1$ $x = 6$ $y = f(6) = 3(5) + 1 = 16$ so $y = 16$

EXAMPLE Determine the domain and the range of a function from a graphed line and its end points.

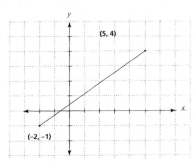

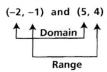

$(-2, -1)$ and $(5, 4)$

Domain $= -2 \leq x \leq 5$
Range $= -1 \leq y \leq 4$

Directions Determine the range for each function with the given domain.

1. $f(x) = 2x + 5$ domain: –1, 0, 3, 7, 10   range: _____   **4.** $f(x) = x^2 + 3x - 4$ domain: –3, 0, 2, 4, 6   range: _____

2. $f(x) = x^3$ domain: –1, 0, 2, 5, 8   range: _____   **5.** $f(x) = 3x - 9$ domain: –4, –3, 0, 1, 8   range: _____

3. $f(x) = \frac{1}{2}x - 2$ domain: $\frac{-1}{2}$, 0, 3, 5, 9   range: _____   **6.** $f(x) = x^2 - x$ domain: –3, –1, 0, 2, 3   range: _____

Directions Determine the domain and the range from the graph and the given ordered pairs.

7. domain: _____   range: _____   **8.** domain: _____   range: _____

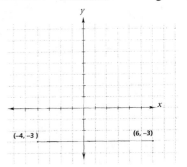

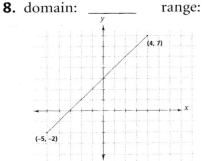

9. domain: _____   range: _____   **10.** domain: _____   range: _____

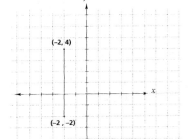

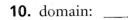

Graphing Lines

| EXAMPLE |

Graph the linear equation $y = 2x + 1$.

Step 1 Make a table of values.

Step 2 Choose three different values for x and solve for y.

Step 3 Draw a coordinate system and plot the points from the table of values. Connect the points, draw arrows at the ends of the line, and label the line $y = 2x + 1$.

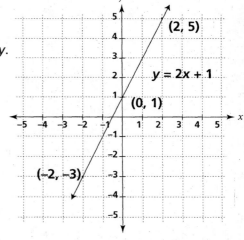

$y = 2x + 1$	
x	y
–2	–3
0	1
2	5

Directions Complete each table of values. Graph the first linear equation here and the others on graph paper.

1.

$y = x + 3$	
x	y

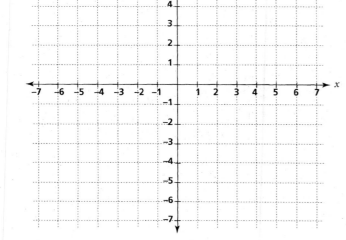

2.

$y = 2x + 4$	
x	y

3.

$y = x - 1$	
x	y

4.

$y = 3x$	
x	y

5.

$y = -x$	
x	y

The Slope of a Line

EXAMPLE

What is the slope of a roof that is 20 feet long and falls 5 feet in that distance?

Step 1 Express the slope as the fraction $\frac{\text{rise}}{\text{run}}$.

Step 2 $\frac{\text{rise}}{\text{run}} = \frac{-5}{+20}$

Step 3 Simplify if possible. $\frac{-5}{+20} = \frac{-1}{4}$

A slope of $\frac{-1}{4}$ means that for every 4 feet of horizontal distance, the roof falls 1 foot.

On a calculator, press –5 ÷ 20. The display shows –0.25.

Directions In this chart, *Distance* is a horizontal measure and *Change in Elevation* is a vertical measure. Use a calculator to find each slope.

Distance	Change in Elevation	Slope
1. 8 mi	6 mi	
2. 80 ft	70 ft	
3. 63.2 yd	151.38 yd	
4. 5.2 m	–3.588 m	
5. 4.2 cm	7.686 cm	
6. 5.1 mm	0.102 mm	
7. 9 in.	–117 in.	
8. 8.1 km	18.225 km	
9. 6.6 yd	6.138 yd	
10. 24 mi	144 mi	
11. 15 m	11.55 m	
12. 13 in.	–416 in.	
13. 6.6 cm	29.04 cm	
14. –8.5 km	2.55 km	
15. 3.25 ft	–83.2 ft	

Formula for the Slope of a Line

EXAMPLE

A line passes through points (0, 0) and (2, 4). Find the slope of the line.

Step 1 Substitute the values for (x_1, y_1) and (x_2, y_2) into the formula $m = \frac{y_2 - y_1}{x_2 - x_1} = \frac{4-0}{2-0} = \frac{4}{2}$.

Remember that points (0, 0) and (2, 4) are written in the form (x_1, y_1) and (x_2, y_2).

Step 2 Simplify. $\frac{4-0}{2-0} = \frac{4}{2} = 2$

The slope of a line passing through points (0, 0) and (2, 4) is 2.

Directions Find the slope of a line that passes through the given points.

1. (0, 2) and (3, 11) _____

2. (4, 12) and (−1, 7) _____

3. (8, 4) and (−6, −3) _____

4. (4, 2) and (−8, −1) _____

5. (5, 4) and (7, −2) _____

6. (−1, 8) and (5, 8) _____

7. (3, 1) and (2, 5) _____

8. (7, 9) and (−5, −1) _____

9. (7, 8) and (0, 3) _____

10. (2, −4) and (6, 3) _____

11. (−3, −3) and (−8, −4) _____

12. (6, 2) and (3, 8) _____

13. (0, 1) and (5, 7) _____

14. (−3, 0) and (1, 8) _____

15. (1, 1) and (5, 9) _____

16. (5, 3) and (9, 2) _____

17. (3, −3) and (4, −5) _____

Directions Answer each question.

18. In a soapbox derby, the first part of a hill has a slope of $\frac{-5}{25}$ and the second part of the hill has a slope of $\frac{-4}{16}$. Which part of the hill has the steeper slope? Explain. _____

19. A bicycle trail has two slopes. The first slope is $\frac{-3}{20}$ and the second slope is $\frac{5}{15}$. Which is the easier to ride? Explain. _____

20. Tae wants to exercise by jogging up a hill. One hill has a slope of $\frac{3}{20}$. Another hill has a slope of $\frac{6}{40}$. Which hill will be more difficult to jog up? Explain. _____

The Slope-Intercept Form of a Line

EXAMPLE   Find the slope, x-intercept, and y-intercept of the line $2y = 6x + 4$.

Step 1 Write $2y = 6x + 4$ in the slope-intercept form by solving for y.

$$\frac{2y}{2} = \frac{6x}{2} + \frac{4}{2} \quad y = 3x + 2$$

Step 2 Determine the slope by looking at the form $y = mx + b$.

$y = 3x + 2$ The slope is 3, since it corresponds to m.

Step 3 Determine the y-intercept by looking at the form $y = mx + b$.

$y = 3x + 2$ The y-intercept is 2, since it corresponds to b.

Step 4 Determine the x-intercept by substituting 0 for y and solving for x.

$y = 3x + 2 \quad 0 = 3x + 2 \quad -3x = 2 \quad x = \frac{-2}{3}$ The x-intercept of the line is $\frac{-2}{3}$.

Directions Identify the slope, x-intercept, and y-intercept of each line.

1.

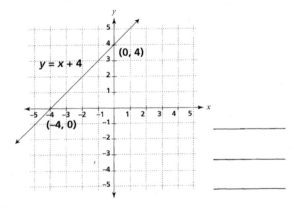

$y = x + 4$

$(0, 4)$

$(-4, 0)$

_____

_____

_____

2.

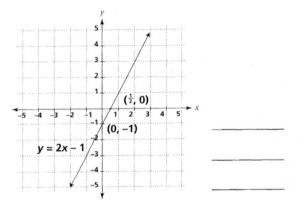

$(\frac{1}{2}, 0)$

$(0, -1)$

$y = 2x - 1$

_____

_____

_____

Directions Write each of these linear equations in slope-intercept form.

3. $4y = 8x + 20$ _____

4. $-y = -x + 8$ _____

5. $2y = -6x + 6$ _____

6. $-3y = 6x + 3$ _____

7. $4y = 4x - 28$ _____

8. $-2y = 2x - 1$ _____

Directions Find the slope, x-intercept, and y-intercept of each line.

9. $y = x - 5$ _____

10. $y = 2x + 4$ _____

11. $y = -3x - 1$ _____

12. $y = x - 2$ _____

13. $y = 4x + 1$ _____

14. $2y = -2x + 6$ _____

15. $-3y = 6x - 15$ _____

Angles and Angle Measures

EXAMPLE

Find the measure of ∠DEF.

Step 1 Place the center of the protractor at the vertex of the angle.

Step 2 Place the 0° line of the protractor along one of the rays in the angle.

Step 3 Read the measure of the angle, counting up from 0°. The measure of ∠DEF = 65°.

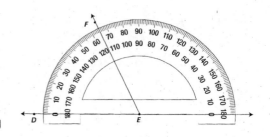

Directions Use the illustration at the right.
Name the rays that make each angle.
Then write the measure of each angle.

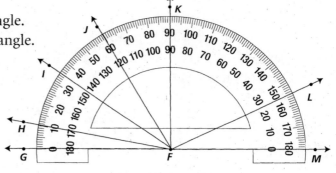

Angle	Rays	Measure
1. GFH	_____	_____
2. GFI	_____	_____
3. GFJ	_____	_____
4. GFK	_____	_____
5. GFL	_____	_____

Angle	Rays	Measure
6. LFM	_____	_____
7. KFM	_____	_____
8. JFM	_____	_____
9. IFM	_____	_____
10. HFM	_____	_____

Identifying and Classifying Angles

EXAMPLE   Name two angles adjacent to ∠LKO.
Name the angle that is vertical to ∠1.

∠OKN and ∠LKM are adjacent to ∠LKO because
they have point K as their vertex and a common
side (LK or OK).

∠1 and ∠3 are vertical angles, because ∠3
is opposite ∠1.

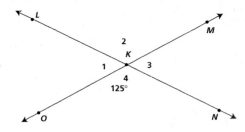

Directions Identify these angles.
Write *adjacent, vertical,
acute,* or *obtuse.* Some angles
may have more than one
description.

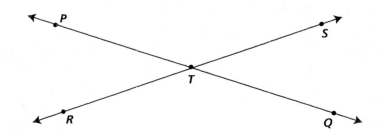

1. ∠PTS and ∠RTQ   _____

2. ∠PTS and ∠STQ   _____

3. ∠PTS   _____

4. ∠PTR   _____

5. ∠RTP and ∠PTS   _____

6. ∠RTP and ∠STQ   _____

7. ∠QTS   _____

8. ∠RTQ   _____

Directions Find the measures.

9. m∠STQ   _____

10. m∠RTQ   _____

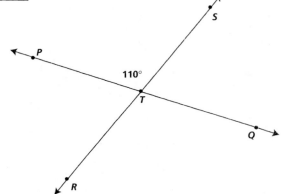

Complementary and Supplementary Angles

EXAMPLE
If the sum of the measures of two angles is 90°, the angles are complementary.

Angles *c* and *d* are complementary. Write an equation to find m∠c.

$m\angle c + 60° = 90°$

$m\angle c = 90° - 60°$

$m\angle c = 30°$

Directions ∠x and ∠y are complementary. Write an equation to find the measure of ∠y.

1. $m\angle x = 50°$ _____ _____

2. $m\angle x = 20°$ _____ _____

3. $m\angle x = 45°$ _____ _____

4. $m\angle x = 30°$ _____ _____

EXAMPLE
If the sum of the measures of two angles is 180°, the angles are supplementary.

Angles *o* and *p* are supplementary. Write an equation to find m∠p.

$m\angle p + 75° = 180°$

$m\angle p = 180° - 75°$

$m\angle p = 105°$

Directions Find the measures.

5. What is the measure of ∠h? _____

6. What is the measure of ∠k? _____

7. What is the measure of ∠i? _____

8. What is the measure of ∠m? _____

9. What is the measure of ∠l? _____

10. What is the measure of ∠n? _____

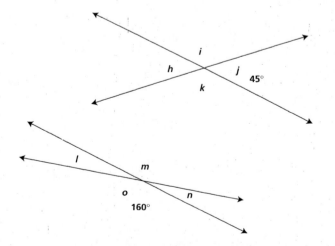

Angle Measure in a Triangle

EXAMPLE

Write an equation to find the missing measure.

$m\angle KLM + 70° = 180°$

$m\angle KLM = 180° - 70°$

$m\angle KLM = 110°$

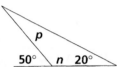

Find $m\angle p$.

$n = 180° - 50°$

$n = 130°$

$130° + 20° + p = 180°$ $p = 30°$

Directions Write an equation to find the missing measure.

1. $m\angle XYZ$ _____

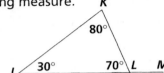

2. $m\angle TUV$ _____

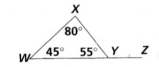

3. $m\angle 1$ _____

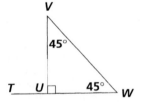

Directions Find the measures.

4. $m\angle a$ _____

$m\angle b$ _____

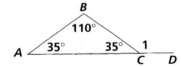

5. $m\angle c$ _____

$m\angle d$ _____

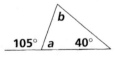

Naming Triangles

Tick marks show whether sides have the same or different lengths.

This triangle has 3 sides of the same length.

This triangle has sides of 3 different lengths.

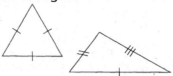

Arcs show whether angles are the same or different.

This triangle has angles with 3 different measures.

A square is used to show a 90° angle.

Directions Write the name of each triangle. Some triangles may have more than one name.

1.

_____

2.

_____

3.

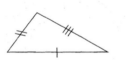

_____

4.

_____

5.

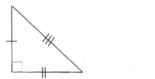

_____

6.

105°

45°

30°

_____

7.

_____

8.

_____

9.

100°

_____

10.

65°

45°   70°

_____

Congruent Triangles

Are these two triangles congruent?
Measure the sides and angles of both triangles.

Label the sides and angles that match. Because the triangles
have two angles and an included side that are equal,
they are congruent. (ASA)

Directions Are the triangles in each pair congruent? Tell why or why not.

1.

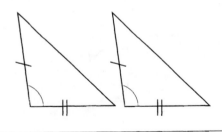

_____

2.

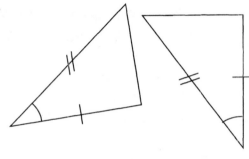

_____

3.

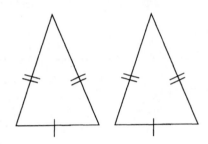

_____

4.

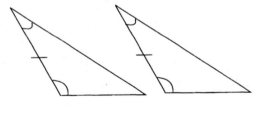

_____

5.

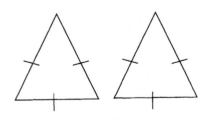

_____

Similar Triangles

$\triangle PLM \sim \triangle PNO$. Study the measurements given. Find m$\angle$N and m$\angle$L. Find the length of $\overline{PO}$.

Step 1 The triangles are similar so the two angles will have the same measurement.

Step 2 m$\angle L$ + 75° + 45° = 180°

m$\angle L$ = 180° − 75° − 45°   m$\angle L$ = 60°

m$\angle N$ = 60°

Step 3 The triangles are similar so the corresponding sides form equal ratios.

Step 4 $\frac{LM}{NO} = \frac{PM}{PO}$

$\frac{4}{2} = \frac{4.8}{PO}$ $PO = 4.8(\frac{2}{4})$

$PO = 2.4$ cm

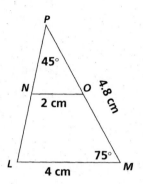

Directions Study the illustrations. Find the measures.

1. m$\angle D$ _____

2. m of $\overline{CB}$ _____

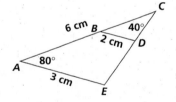

3. m$\angle K$ _____

4. m of $\overline{IJ}$ _____

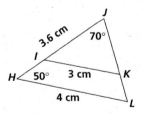

5. m$\angle T$ _____

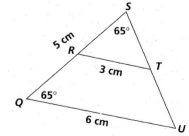

Parallelograms

EXAMPLE

Describe the properties of this quadrilateral. Then name it.

       All sides are the same length.

       It has 2 pairs of parallel sides.

       The opposite sides are the same length.

       The opposite angles are equal.

       It is a rhombus.

Directions   Name two properties of each figure. Then name the figure.

1.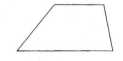

_____

_____

2.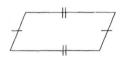

_____

_____

3.

_____

_____

4.

_____

_____

5.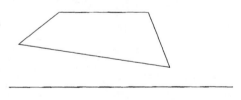

_____

_____

6.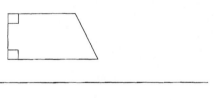

_____

_____

Directions   Tell whether each statement is *true* or *false*.

7. A rhombus is also a parallelogram.   _____

8. A parallelogram is also a quadrilateral.   _____

9. A trapezoid is also a rhombus.   _____

10. A square is also a rectangle.   _____

Quadrilaterals and Diagonals

EXAMPLE

Use the Pythagorean theorem to find the length of the diagonal.
Use a scientific calculator and round your answer to the nearest hundredth.

$$a^2 + b^2 = c^2$$
$$2^2 + 5^2 = c^2$$
$$4 + 25 = c^2$$
$$\sqrt{29} = c^2$$
$$5.39 = c$$

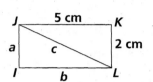

Directions Answer the questions about these rectangles. Use a scientific calculator and round your answer to the nearest hundredth.

1. What is the length of *MN*? _____

2. Use the Pythagorean theorem to find *c*. _____

3. Is △*NMP* congruent to △*NPO*? _____

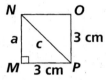

4. What is the m∠*R*? Explain. _____

_____

5. What is the length of *ST*? _____

6. Find the length of *SQ*. _____

7. What would be the length of *RT*? _____

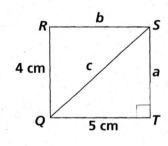

8. What is the length of *VW*? _____

9. What is m∠*VUX*? _____

10. Is △*VUX* congruent to △*VXW*? _____

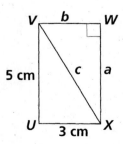

Polygons and Diagonals

EXAMPLE Find the sum of the measures of the angles and the measure
of each interior and exterior angle.

To find the sum of all the angle measures in a regular hexagon:

$(6 - 2)180° = a$

$(4)180° = a$

$720° = a$

To find the measure of each interior angle:

$\frac{720°}{6} = 120°$

To find the measure of each exterior angle:

$120° + e = 180°$

$e = 180° - 120°$

$e = 60°$

Directions Find the measures of these regular polygons.

1. m∠6

_____

2. m∠e

_____

3. The sum of all interior angles

_____

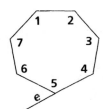

---

4. m∠8

_____

5. m∠e

_____

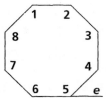

Reflections in the Coordinate Plane

EXAMPLE

Reflect the image over the *x*-axis.

Reflected points:

$A' = (0, -2)$

$B' = (5, -2)$

$C' = (3, -5)$

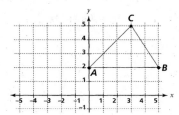

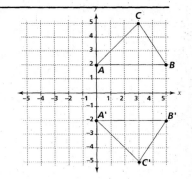

Directions   Reflect each image over the specified axis.
Give the coordinates of the image vertices.

1. Line of reflection = *x*-axis   **2.** Line of reflection = *y*-axis   **3.** Line of reflection = *x*-axis

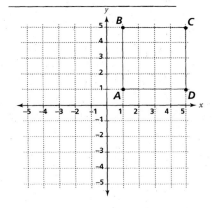

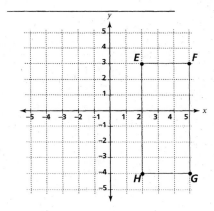

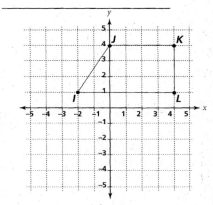

4. Line of reflection = *x*-axis   **5.** Line of reflection = *y*-axis

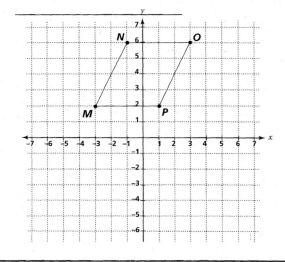

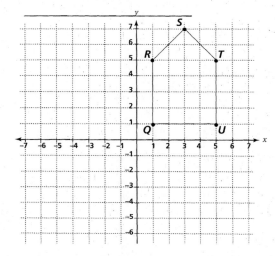

Reflections Over Different Lines

EXAMPLE

Reflect the image over the specified line of reflection: $x = 2$
Give the coordinates of the image vertices.

Reflected points:

$A' = (1, 3)$

$B' = (-1, 3)$

$C' = (-1, 1)$

$D' = (1, 1)$

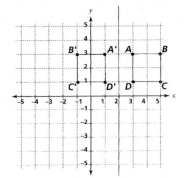

Directions Reflect each image over the specified line of reflection.
Give the coordinates of the image vertices.

1. Line of reflection $x = 3$

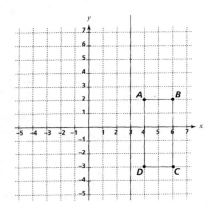

2. Line of reflection $y = 1$

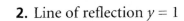
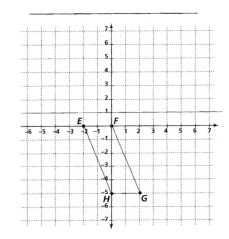

3. Line of reflection $x = -1$

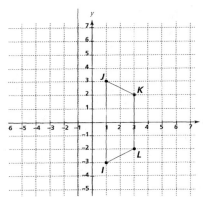

4. Line of reflection $x = 2$

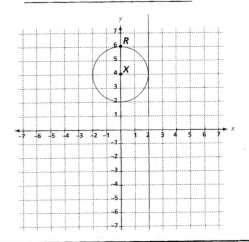

5. Line of reflection $y = -2$

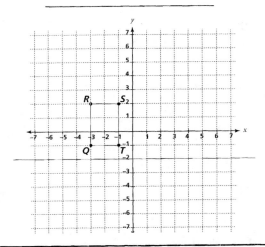

Special Reflections: Symmetries

| EXAMPLE | Find the line of symmetry in the letter *A*. | A | The letter *A* has a vertical line of symmetry. | |

Directions   Draw any lines of symmetry that the following letters have.

1.   Y

2.   M

3.   O

4.   B

5.   D

6.   W

7.   X

8.   C

9.   F

10.   H

Slides and Translations

EXAMPLE   Name the image point when the object point (3, 4) is mapped by the following translation.

$$(x, y) \rightarrow (x - 2, y - 5)$$

Image point = (1, −1)

Directions   Name the image point when the object point (4, 4) is mapped by the following translations.

1. $(x, y) \rightarrow (x - 4, y + 2)$ _____

2. $(x, y) \rightarrow (x + 1, y - 1)$ _____

3. $(x, y) \rightarrow (x - 6, y - 3)$ _____

4. $(x, y) \rightarrow (x + 3, y + 1)$ _____

Directions   Name the image point when the object point (−2, 1) is mapped by the following translations.

5. $(x, y) \rightarrow (x - 2, y + 1)$ _____

6. $(x, y) \rightarrow (x - 5, y - 1)$ _____

7. $(x, y) \rightarrow (x + 4, y + 3)$ _____

8. $(x, y) \rightarrow (x - 2, y + 3)$ _____

Directions   Name the image point when the object point (−7, 3) is mapped by the following translations.

9. $(x, y) \rightarrow (x + 24, y - 4)$ _____

10. $(x, y) \rightarrow (x - 1, y - 1)$ _____

11. $(x, y) \rightarrow (x + 5, y - 3)$ _____

12. $(x, y) \rightarrow (x - 3, y + 1)$ _____

Directions   Identify the image of (x, y) under the following translations. Remember, the image takes the form $(x + a, y + b)$.

13. $(-4, 5) \rightarrow (-6, 2)$ _____

14. $(1, 2) \rightarrow (4, 8)$ _____

15. $(-2, -3) \rightarrow (3, 4)$ _____

Rotations

Rotate the following image 90° clockwise around point *O*.

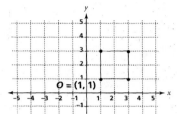

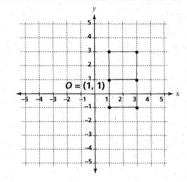

Directions Copy the given figure onto graph paper. Then rotate the object 90° clockwise around point *O* to produce an image. Draw the image.

1.

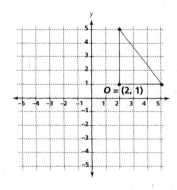

2.

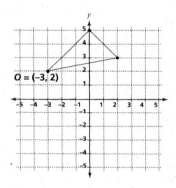

3.

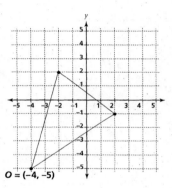

4.

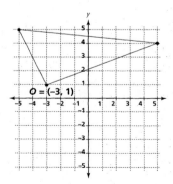

5.

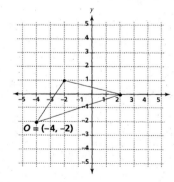

Bar Graphs

EXAMPLE

A bar graph uses rectangular bars to organize and display data. It is made up of these individual parts:

- a title
- a horizontal axis with labels
- a vertical axis with labels
- an interval
- data

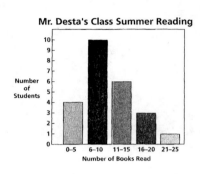

Directions Suppose you were asked to construct a bar graph that organizes and displays the data shown in this table. The table shows the results of a class election for president.

Election Results	
Candidate A	10 votes
Candidate B	12 votes
Candidate C	4 votes

1. What title would you choose for the bar graph?

_____

2. What label would you choose for the horizontal axis?

_____

3. What label would you choose for the vertical axis?

_____

4. What interval would you use? Explain.

_____

5. Use your answers from problems 1–4 to construct a bar graph for the data on your own paper.

Frequency Tables

EXAMPLE

Suppose two 1–6 number cubes are tossed at the same time and the outcomes of the cubes are added to create a sum.

For example, if the outcome on the first cube is 3 and the outcome on the second cube is 4, the sum of the outcomes is 3 + 4 or 7.

This frequency table shows the number of different ways various sums can be made by tossing two 1–6 number cubes.

Outcome Sum	Tally	Frequency
2	I	1
3	II	2
4	III	3
5	IIII	4
6	IIII I	5
7	IIII I	6
8	IIII	5
9	IIII	4
10	III	3
11	II	2
12	I	1

Directions Answer these questions about the frequency table in the example.

1. What is the greatest possible sum that can be created by tossing two 1–6 number cubes? Explain how that sum can be created.

_____

2. What is the least possible sum that can be created by tossing two 1–6 number cubes? Explain how that sum can be created.

_____

3. How many tosses of the number cubes are shown in the data? Tell how you know.

_____

4. Based on the data, which sum will occur most often when two 1–6 number cubes are tossed? Which sums will occur least often?

_____

5. What interval was used to create this frequency table? Is there a better interval that could have been used? Explain.

_____

Circle Graphs

EXAMPLE   A circle graph uses parts of a circle to organize and display data.

The part of this graph labeled 65% makes up 234° of the graph because 65% of 360° = 0.65 • 360° = 234°.

The part of this graph labeled 35% makes up 126° of the graph because 35% of 360° = 0.35 • 360° = 126°.

You can check your work by finding the sum of the parts.

234° + 126° = 360° ✔

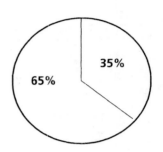

Directions   Study this circle graph. Answer the questions that follow.

1. Name the fraction in simplest form, the decimal, and the number of degrees that represent Part A of the graph.

   _____

2. Name the fraction in simplest form, the decimal, and the number of degrees that represent Part B of the graph.

   _____

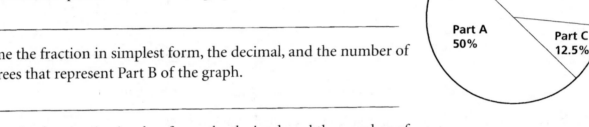

3. Name the fraction in simplest form, the decimal, and the number of degrees that represent Part C of the graph.

   _____

4. Describe how a circle graph can be checked for accuracy.

   _____

   _____

5. In the graph, suppose that Part A represents 500 votes. How many votes altogether are represented by the graph?

   _____

Histograms

EXAMPLE   Draw a histogram for the number of times tails is obtained when 4 dimes are tossed 20 times.

Frequency Table	
# of Tails	Frequency
0	4
1	3
2	3
3	8
4	2
Total	20

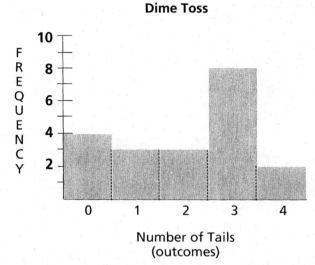

Dime Toss

Directions   A 1–6 number cube is rolled 20 times. Use the frequency table below to create a histogram of the results. Be sure to include a title and label the vertical and horizontal axes.

Frequency Table	
Result	Frequency
1	2
2	3
3	4
4	1
5	7
6	3
Total	20

Scatterplots

| EXAMPLE | Use the data to create a scatterplot. |

Ages of Spouses		
	Spouse A	**Spouse B**
Pair 1	24	27
Pair 2	35	32
Pair 3	51	47
Pair 4	43	43
Pair 5	26	31

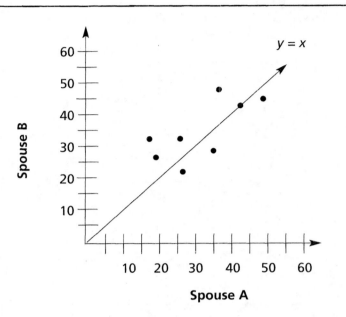

Directions   Design a scatterplot for the following data.

Miles Jogged This Week		
	Jogger A	**Jogger B**
Pair 1	12	15
Pair 2	21	9
Pair 3	18	18
Pair 4	23	26
Pair 5	6	6
Pair 6	11	8

Mean

EXAMPLE

Study the data shown in the table. The data show the average amount of precipitation received each month in Miami, Florida.

Month	Precipitation in Inches	Month	Precipitation in Inches
January	2.0	July	5.7
February	2.1	August	7.6
March	2.4	September	7.6
April	2.9	October	5.6
May	6.2	November	2.7
June	9.3	December	1.8

To find the mean of a set of data, find the sum of the data values in the set, then divide by the number of data values.

Directions Answer these questions about the data table in the example.

1. What useful information do the labels in the table provide?

_____

2. How many data values does the set of data contain? _____

3. What is the sum of the data values? _____

4. Identify the steps to follow to determine the mean of the set of data.

_____

_____

5. What is the mean amount of precipitation received each month in Miami, Florida? Round your answer to the nearest hundredth inch.

_____

Median

EXAMPLE

Study the data shown in the table.
The data show the inauguration ages
of some U.S. presidents.

The median of a set of data is the middle
value when the set is ordered from greatest
to least or least to greatest. To find the mean
of a set of data, order the values in the set
from greatest to least or least to greatest.
Cross off the greatest and least values in the set.
The median is the middle data value, or the
mean of the two middle values.

President	Inauguration Age (in years)
Washington	57
Jefferson	57
Lincoln	52
Harrison	55
Cleveland	55
McKinley	54
Wilson	56
Hoover	54
L. Johnson	55
Carter	52

Directions Answer these questions about the data table in the example.

1. Order the data values from greatest to least or from least to greatest.

   _____

2. Does the set of data have an even number or an odd number of data values?

   _____

3. How is finding the median of a data set with an even number of values different from finding the median of a data set with an odd number of values?

   _____

   _____

4. What is the median inauguration age of the presidents shown in the table?

   _____

5. President Bill Clinton was 46 years old at inauguration, and President Truman was 60 years old. Suppose these two presidents were added to the table. Would the median change? If so, to what?

   _____

Mode

Study the data shown in the table. The data show elevation in feet above sea level of selected U.S. cities.

The mode of a set of data is the value or values that occur most often. To determine the mode of a set of data, count the number of times each value appears. The value or values that appear most often are the mode.

City	Elevation Above Sea Level (in feet)
San Diego, CA	20
Bellingham, WA	60
Galveston, TX	5
Cambridge, MA	20
Orlando, FL	70
Wilmington, NC	35
New Haven, CT	40
Baltimore, MD	20
Key West, FL	5
Albany, NY	20

Directions Answer these questions about the data table in the example.

1. What useful information do the labels in the table provide?

   _____

2. How many different data values appear in the table? What are those values?

   _____

3. How could you determine the mode of the data?

   _____

4. What is the mode of the data?

   _____

5. Suppose each value in a set of data occurs the same number of times. What is the mode of the set of data?

   _____

Range

EXAMPLE

Study the data shown in the table. The data show the lengths in miles of selected rivers in North America.

The range of a set of data is the difference between the greatest and least values.

River	Length (miles)
Missouri	2,315
Kentucky	259
Arkansas	1,459
Milk	625
Porcupine	569
Snake	1,038
Mississippi	2,340
White	722
Yukon	1,979
Pecos	926

Directions Answer these questions about the data table in the example.

1. What is the longest river shown in the table? What is its length?

_____

2. What is the shortest river shown in the table? What is its length?

_____

3. How could you determine the range of the data?

_____

4. What is the range of the data?

_____

5. In order to find the range of a set of data, is it necessary to order data in a set from greatest to least or from least to greatest? Explain.

_____

_____

Data and Statistics

Study the data shown in this table. The data show the locations and heights in feet of famous waterfalls.

Waterfall	Location	Height (in feet)
Panther	Alberta, Canada	600
Multnomah	Oregon, U.S.	620
Augrabies	South Africa	480
Feather	California, U.S.	640
Marina	Guyana	500
Bridalveil	Yosemite National Park, U.S.	620

Directions Answer these questions about the data table in the example.

1. What data are represented in the table? _____

2. How many data values does the table display? _____

3. Suppose you were asked to display the data using a bar graph. What interval would you use? Explain.

_____

4. When should you break the vertical axis of a bar graph? Explain.

_____

5. Would it be easy or difficult to display the waterfall data in a circle graph? Tell why.

_____

6. Is a frequency table the best way to organize and display the data in the table? Tell why or why not.

_____

7. Find the mean of the data. Round your answer to the nearest whole number. _____

8. Find the median of the data. _____

9. Find the mode of the data. _____

10. Find the range of the data. _____

Box-and-Whiskers Plots

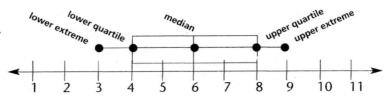

EXAMPLE
Study the data shown in
this box-and-whiskers plot.

To construct a box-and-whiskers plot:

- Find the median of the entire set of data. Label this value *median.*
- Find the median of all values below the median. Label this value *lower quartile.*
- Find the median of all values above the median. Label this value *upper quartile.*
- Find the least value in the set of data. Label this value *lower extreme.*
- Find the greatest value in the set of data. Label this value *upper extreme.*

Directions Use the set of data shown below for problems 1–5.

{16 19 11 23 15 18 22 17 10 12 21}

1. Order the data in the set from greatest to least or from least to greatest.

_____

2. What is the median of the set of data? _____

3. What value represents the lower quartile? _____   The upper quartile? _____

4. What value represents the lower extreme? _____   The upper extreme? _____

5. Construct a box-and-whiskers plot of the data using this number line.

```
◄──┼──┼──┼──┼──┼──┼──┼──┼──┼──┼──┼──┼──┼──┼──┼──┼──┼──┼──┼──┼──►
    5  6  7  8  9  10 11 12 13 14 15 16 17 18 19 20 21 22 23 24 25
```

Name _____ Date _____ Period _____

The Probability Fraction

EXAMPLE

Consider the frequency table that shows the number of different ways various sums can be made by tossing two 1–6 number cubes.

When two 1–6 number cubes are tossed at the same time, 36 different outcomes are possible.

Outcome Sum	Tally	Frequency
2			1
3				2
4					3
5						4
6	++++	5
7	++++		6
8	++++	5
9						4
10					3
11				2
12			1

Directions Use the probability fraction $P = \dfrac{\text{number of favorable outcomes}}{\text{number of possible outcomes}}$ and the frequency table to find each of the following probabilities. Whenever possible, express your answer in simplest form.

1. $P(10)$ _____

2. $P(5)$ _____

3. $P(3)$ _____

4. $P(12)$ _____

5. P (an even sum) _____

6. P (an odd sum) _____

7. Which outcome shown in the table is most likely? _____

8. Which outcomes are least likely? _____

9. Which outcome is twice as likely as an outcome of 4? _____

Which outcomes are $\frac{1}{3}$ as likely as an outcome of 7? _____

10. Some board games require a player to roll two number cubes. How might knowing the probability of which sums are more likely to occur help you become a better board game player?

_____

_____

Dependent and Independent Events

EXAMPLE   Suppose 2 children take one pencil each from the same box of 10 pencils. Half of the pencils have erasers, half do not. The first child chooses a pencil, then the second child chooses. What is the probability that both will choose a pencil with an eraser?

These events are dependent.

- The probability of an eraser for child A's choice is $\frac{5}{10}$, or $\frac{1}{2}$.

- The probability of an eraser for child B's choice is $\frac{5-1}{10-1}$, or $\frac{4}{9}$.

Suppose instead that each child chooses from an identical separate box of pencils. These events are independent, so each probability is identical.

Directions   Write whether the events are *dependent* or *independent*.

1. Each of 5 children chooses and keeps a marble from a bag of 5 marbles.   _____

2. A player in a board game rolls a number cube. Then a different player rolls the cube.   _____

3. A clothing store has one of a particular shirt left. One man buys the shirt. Then another man comes in, asking to buy the same shirt.   _____

4. Three children always sit on the backseat of their family car. Today, the first child sits in the middle. Then the second child sits down.   _____

5. One person draws a card from the deck, looks at it, and puts it back into the deck. The next person then draws from the deck.   _____

6. At the start of a board game, one person selects her playing piece from a bag of 7 pieces. Then you select your piece.   _____

7. A grab bag holds 3 wrapped gifts: one red, one blue, and one green. You take the gift wrapped in red. Then the person on your right takes one.   _____

8. A friend shows you a card trick, having you select 1 card out of 5. Then your friend repeats the same trick with someone else.   _____

9. Two trains are on the same track line. Train number one slows down. Train number two then slows down.   _____

10. A vase in a flower shop holds 3 flowers. After you take one, the florist replaces it. Then another person takes one.   _____

The Fundamental Principle of Counting

EXAMPLE

These combinations show all of the different ways the letters *a*, *b*, and *c* can be arranged if the letters cannot be used more than once in any arrangement.

abc   *acb*   *bac*   *bca*   *cab*   *cba*

Another way to determine the number of different ways the letters can be arranged is to use the fundamental principle of counting. It states that three letters can be arranged 3 • 2 • 1 or 6 different ways.

Directions Use the fundamental principle of counting or draw a diagram to determine the number of arrangements in each of the following problems.

1. How many different ways can two students seat themselves in two chairs?

   _____

2. How many different four-digit whole numbers can be made using the digits 1, 3, 5, and 7 if the digits can appear only once in each number?

   _____

3. Angela is choosing a skirt and a blouse to wear from five skirts and four blouses. How many different combinations of one skirt and one blouse does Angela have to choose from?

   _____

4. Suppose the 1–6 number cube and the spinner shown below are each used once. How many different outcomes are possible?

   _____

5. How many different three-digit numbers are possible when each spinner shown below is spun once? The left spinner will provide the first digit of the number, the center spinner will provide the second digit, and the right spinner will provide the third digit.

   _____

   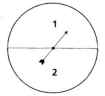 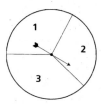 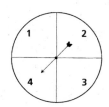
